Contents

JAMES P. CANNON FEBRUARY 11, 1890–AUGUST 21, 1974

James P. Cannon died at the age of eighty-four of a heart attack August 21 at his home in Los Angeles. By coincidence, August 21 marked the thirty-fourth anniversary of the death of Leon Trotsky.

Cannon was a founding member of the Communist party in the United States, and was a founder and leader of the world Trotskyist movement. His political life spanned sixty-six years of participation in the class struggle—from the pre-World War I socialist movement to the radicalization of the 1960s and 1970s. At the time of his death he was national chairman emeritus of the Socialist Workers party.

At the age of twenty-one, Cannon joined the Industrial Workers of the World, becoming a skilled agitator and organizer. In the example set by Eugene V. Debs and other leading opponents of imperialist war, he refused to support the slaughter of World War I. As a member of the left wing of the Socialist party, he hailed the victory of the Russian revolution in 1917.

As a member of the American section of the Third International, he learned from the Bolsheviks what kind of party was necessary to carry the revolutionary struggle to victory—a fighting, disciplined, democratic party based on a clearcut Marxist program.

When the Stalinist bureaucracy arose in the Soviet Union, Cannon rejected its doctrine of "socialism in one country," and after his expulsion from the Communist party in 1928, founded *The Militant* with a handful of co-thinkers who became the nucleus of the future Socialist Workers party. In 1938 Cannon and others collaborated with Trotsky in establishing the Fourth International, the World Party of the Socialist Revolution.

Together with other members of the SWP, he was sentenced to prison because of political opposition to the war aims of U. S. imperialism. Cannon emerged from prison in 1945, after serving a year and twenty days of a sixteen-month sentence, to help lead the party through the postwar upsurge and the subsequent witch-hunt of the 1950s. While many other revolutionists became discouraged and turned away from Marxism in that period, Cannon remained confident that the United States was subject to the same historical laws as other capitalist states and would one day witness the revolutionary rise of the working class.

The leadership team he helped forge held the party together in anticipation of a more favorable political climate. This began to appear in the 1960s. The 1,250 socialists who, at the time of his death, were gathered in Oberlin, Ohio, for the 1974 Socialist Activists and Educational Conference testify to the success of his effort to lay a solid basis for a revolutionary-socialist party in the United States.

In the tradition of the American Trotskyist movement, the conference at Oberlin held a "Political Tribute to Jim Cannon," at which party leaders and activists who had worked with Cannon during his long career paid homage to his contributions to the socialist movement.

Speakers at the meeting were Jack Barnes, national chairman of the Socialist Workers party; Karolyn Kerry, a comrade and co-worker of Cannon's for forty years; Andrew Pulley, national chairman of the Young Socialist Alliance; Peggy Brundy, one of a team of comrades who lived in the Cannon household during the last few years, sharing the chores and helping organize Cannon's work; Joseph Hansen, the editor of *Intercontinental Press*; and George Novack, collaborator with Cannon in the revolutionary-socialist movement for forty-one years.

By the time the meeting of tribute was held,

messages and telegrams from Cannon's comrades and friends had begun to arrive from around the world.

The Oberlin meeting concluded by launching a financial campaign—the James P. Cannon Party-Building Fund—to help move forward the struggle to build the revolutionary-socialist party to which Cannon dedicated his life. Participants at the meeting contributed or pledged more than $50,000 toward this effort.

JACK BARNES: 'JIM ALWAYS REMAINED TRUE TO HIS REBEL YOUTH'

The announcement of Cannon's death was made at a conference assembly the morning of Aug. 22 by Jack Barnes, national secretary of the Socialist Workers Party. The following are excerpts from his remarks.

I must begin this morning by telling you something important. Jim Cannon died last night in Los Angeles.

He went quickly with a heart attack, in the early evening after a fruitful day at *work*, cogitating and talking to comrades.

Tomorrow night we want to hold here a special tribute meeting to Jim, with all the comrades gathered. Comrade Joe Hansen will be the main speaker and will tell about the life and the meaning of the life of Jim Cannon. And at the same time we will launch a James P. Cannon Party-Building Fund, to carry forward the work he wanted.

Jim would have been 85 years old this coming February. Eighty-five. He lived a wonderful and fruitful as well as long life. He said it wasn't always easy and comfortable, but he was a proletarian revolutionist with a lot of Wobbly blood, so that was all right. And it was certainly rewarding, beyond imagination.

If our estimate is correct, almost 70 of Jim's years were as a conscious revolutionist: beginning as a teenager revolting against the injustices and the frame-ups of leaders of the labor movement and the oppressed; being influenced by the class he came from, the working class, and a socialist father; and learning from the Russian revolution how to bring about this goal. He never turned back from this. He remained, as he said he tried to be, completely true to his rebel youth.

You all remember what Theodore Draper said in his introduction to Jim's book, *The First Ten Years of American Communism*—he said that Jim remembered so well, unlike anyone else, because he *wanted* to and he had absolutely no reason not to.

Cannon in January 1926, while serving as the Secretary of the International Labor Defense.

The whole week here has been a tribute to Jim. Jim, in what he thought and did and taught us, is everywhere—in the books we study and the ones we're planning, in all the speeches at this conference, and in the themes we developed. Even some of the sentences we used, and arguments and lessons, were directly from him. Our decision to launch the prepaid subscription cards as part of our *Militant* circulation drive was an idea that Jim had been campaigning for.

Up to the last interviews he gave—and he gave

several in the last few weeks—he spent his time discussing the socialist perspective and exactly the same questions we discussed here. And he had come to one of the same conclusions we have come to: that we are entering a period in this country where all things are possible if we do our job.

Jim really loved the idea of these socialist educational conferences. He wished the party had more resources and could have done more of this earlier. He told me it was "the gathering of the clan," and that this was important because through such gatherings we learn how to think together and to know each other from all around the country and the world, and we learn to have confidence in each other. And that more than anything else, he thought, was the key to the future of the party.

So we're going to do what he would want us to do and what he taught us to do. We're going to go ahead, take care of business—humanity's most important business—the building of the revolutionary party and the revolutionary international.

JOSEPH HANSEN:
'JIM FORGED THE NUCLEUS OF THE REVOLUTIONARY PARTY IN THE U.S.'

The Aug. 23 Political Tribute to Jim Cannon was chaired by Jack Barnes, who described the purpose of the meeting as "to begin the process of paying tribute to Jim Cannon's 70 years of revolutionary activity, and to celebrate the imperishable things that he gave us, his party, on a national and world scale."

The main speaker of the evening was Joseph Hansen, member of the political committee of the Socialist Workers Party and editor of *Intercontinental Press*. Barnes noted that for both Joe Hansen and Reba Hansen, "1974 is the fortieth year of collaboration and friendship with Jim Cannon in building the revolutionary party."

"Maybe Joe and Reba knew James Patrick Cannon, the person, better than almost anyone," Barnes stated. "Even more important, they learned from him, especially, about team leadership and work—as Jim always emphasized, hard work."

Barnes continued: "Joe Hansen is one of the longstanding older members of the SWP leadership team forged by Jim and, in my opinion, the outstanding leader today of the Fourth International, which Jim Cannon helped found." (The Socialist Workers Party is now prevented by reactionary legislation from organizationally affiliating with the Fourth International but maintains fraternal political relations.)

The following is Joe Hansen's speech to the meeting.

Jim's life was so bound up with the life of the generation I belong to that it is difficult to speak about him briefly. The mass of material, particularly the flood of memories, is simply too great. I will confine myself to making only a few observations about his development as a revolutionist and his achievements.

At the age of eighty-four, after sixty-six years of service in the revolutionary socialist movement,

Jim's mind was still sharp and lucid. He followed world events closely, kept up with the current literature of the radical movement, remained on top of developments in the Socialist Workers Party and the Young Socialist Alliance, and was keenly interested in the affairs of the Fourth International, holding strong opinions on the current differences being debated in the world party of the socialist revolution.

His advice and judgments will be sorely missed. They were always advanced with complete objectivity and with the interests of the movement as a whole uppermost in his considerations.

Jim was born in Rosedale, Kansas, on February 11, 1890. The family, of Irish background, was an ordinary one except for politics. His father was a socialist and a partisan of the *Appeal to Reason*, a socialist journal of wide circulation and great popularity. A father holding socialist views was an enormous advantage to a boy growing up in the backward Middle West.

A direct result was that at the age of eighteen, Jim joined the Socialist Party. Three years later he joined the Industrial Workers of the World, dual membership being quite common and an accepted practice.

In those years, the United States was experiencing a great radical upsurge. It was a time of bitter strike struggles and violent confrontations with strikebreakers and the police. Under the leadership of Eugene V. Debs, the Socialist Party grew by leaps and bounds, striking deep roots in the labor movement.

Class-conscious battler

Jim was formed as a class-conscious battler in this period, coming to the attention of such superlative fighters and organizers as Vincent St. John, from whom Jim learned invaluable lessons.

In high school, Jim starred in debating, a campus sport of much higher standing than it is today. Participation on the debating team gave Jim a good start in achieving one of his ambitions, which was to become a skilled public speaker.

He made a study of public speaking, observing the celebrities who came to town on lecture tours, reading books on technique, and doing his best to eliminate the speech defects that come natural in the Middle West. This was coupled with practical experience in soapboxing, which is a very hard school. One of the results was that he became renowned by the early twenties in the Communist movement as a highly gifted speaker.

He followed a similar course of study in writing, training himself in this field by seeing how others did it, and reading what he could find on the subject. At one time he began a novel.

In both writing and speaking he tended to be a perfectionist, continually working over his drafts and seeking to bring them to a high polish.

Thus as an organizer, a speaker, and a writer he already had solid skills when he became editor of the *Workers' World* in Kansas City in 1919 at the age of twenty-nine and of *The Toiler*, a Communist Party publication, the following year.

In his ability to present the fundamental concepts and goals of revolutionary socialism in popular terms, Jim had few equals. He was an artist in this field. Many of the short articles he wrote over the years in his column *The Notebook of an Agitator* can be taken as models of revolutionary journalism.

The IWW and the left wing of the Socialist Party in the years leading up to World War I constituted a good training ground for an activist. The lessons remained with Jim throughout the rest of his life.

But the greatest single influence in his political education was the Russian revolution, particularly the October 1917 overturn in which the Bolsheviks under Lenin and Trotsky won power.

That great event, which caught the imagination of class-conscious workers throughout the world as a living example of how to topple capitalism, inspired a whole new generation of revolutionists. For Jim, as for many of his comrades, it became an advanced school in which they were reeducated in some respects and in others received graduate training in theory and in politics.

And they learned in a very practical school. That was the assemblage which came together to found the Communist Party of the United States, in which Jim participated. It included the left wing of the Socialist Party, all the rebels in the IWW who could be convinced, and others. Jim was elected to the new party's Central Committee at the Bridgman, Michigan, convention in 1920.

It was in this school that Jim completed his basic education as a revolutionist. It was under the direct tutelage of the Russians, in conjunction with living experience in the American class struggle in the twenties, that Jim's main talent flowered and he emerged as a political organizer of the highest caliber.

The capitalist class nearly always has talented political organizers at its disposal, some of them coming from wealthy families that specialize in offering political leadership. They are rather rare in the working class, one reason being that many with the talent for it are drawn into serving the capitalist parties. A person with talent in this field must be capable of great dedication and capacity for self-sacrifice to take up the cause of the working class and to remain devoted to it for decades and even a lifetime.

Jim was such a person. It came natural to him

to size up a situation correctly, to take into account the main forces, to judge accurately what ought to be done next, and to win others to these insights. Jim became a skilled technician in working out the best ways of responding to attacks on the revolutionary movement and of mounting effective counteroffensives.

In the twenties in the Communist movement, Jim was justly famed for this. It was the development of this talent in particular that won him a place as one of the key leaders of the Communist Party.

In those days, the Communist Party was something of a jungle—that is, as far as the internal struggles were concerned. At first, the Communist International under Lenin and Trotsky could play a role in ameliorating the situation and helping the comrades to learn the correct lessons from their mistakes.

But later on the Comintern degenerated and itself became a real jungle, in which Jim was one of the best of the jungle fighters. He made errors which he later learned from and never forgot.

Principled politics

The main difference between Jim and some of the others who also had talents along this line was that Jim operated within the framework of principles, the principles of revolutionary socialism. He sought to win, naturally. But his perspective was the long-range one of winning the final battle; that is, the final battle in the struggle to topple capitalism and to replace it with socialism on a world scale.

In his opinion this was a great perspective, the only one really worth a lifetime of effort. He saw it, too, as a realistic perspective, one that would inevitably be realized even if it required the combined efforts of several successive generations of revolutionists.

Jim was an internationalist to the marrow of his bones. He absorbed the internationalist view in his youth as a member of the Socialist Party and of the IWW. The Russian revolution offered living confirmation of the correctness of this outlook.

On top of this, Jim began gaining direct experience in international problems. In addition to the incessant discussions, debates, and factional struggles in the Communist Party of the twenties, Jim served as a delegate to the important Fourth Congress of the Communist International and later to the Sixth, where Stalin sought to smash Trotsky's defense of the program of Leninism.

The Sixth Congress of the Communist International in 1928 marked an important step in the development of James P. Cannon as a political figure of international stature. It was at that congress that he decided to take up the cause represented by Leon Trotsky.

In the previous period he had become deeply disturbed by pernicious moves made by the Comintern in the internal affairs of the American Communist Party. But he did not connect these with the struggle over "Trotskyism" in the Russian party. In fact, from the available information, he was inclined to disregard that struggle and even give the benefit of the doubt to Stalin.

At the Sixth Congress, he and Maurice Spector of the Canadian Communist Party accidentally received copies of an English translation of part of Trotsky's criticism of the draft program that was proposed for adoption at the congress. The rest is history.

The document completely convinced Cannon. He decided to battle for Trotsky's criticisms—not because of any hope of immediate success, but because he saw that Trotsky was *right*.

Not an easy decision

It was not an easy decision. Cannon realized, perhaps better than anyone outside of the Russian Trotskyists, that it would mean ostracism, the breakup of old friendships, and the end of personal relations with many comrades he had known in common battles for years.

However, it was politically necessary to make the turn. For Jim this consideration was paramount. Nothing personal could be permitted to stand in the way of moving ahead in defense of Trotsky's position and against Stalin's bureaucratic gang.

Cannon's decision offers a striking example of the importance of achieving political clarity in a factional struggle. Stalin understood that too. That was why he tried to gag Trotsky and why he eventually used assassination to silence Trotsky's powerful voice.

Thus at a crucial moment, when Trotsky was exiled in far-off Alma-Ata, blocked by force from defending his positions and from answering the most poisonous lies and slanders, one of the main leaders of the American Communist Party joined Trotsky in defense of the program of Leninism, determined to do everything he could to organize a principled faction to struggle for that program on an international scale in the Communist movement.

That decision marked the real beginning of our movement in the United States, although some anticipatory moves in that direction had been taken previously by figures like Antoinette Konikow in Boston. And that decision also marked a banner day for the worldwide movement that eventually became the Fourth International.

James P. Cannon came in on the ground floor in 1928 in the international struggle against Stalinism. He lived to see the Stalinist monolith shattered.

Collaboration with Trotsky

The collaboration between Cannon and Trotsky was particularly fruitful. Some of the detractors of our movement have pictured Cannon as a "yes man," wholly dependent on the ideas furnished by Trotsky, serving only to execute them. I can think of worse relationships; but this picture happens to be inaccurate. It actually maligns Trotsky as much as it does Cannon.

In his relations with Cannon, as in his relations with his secretaries and all members of the staff that worked with him, Trotsky's status was that of an equal. Give-and-take was easy. Trotsky elicited ideas from others and their tendency was to respond, and sometimes to rise above themselves.

This collaboration was, of course, on the political level. The team was not a group of compatible souls drawn together out of common personal predilections, tastes, and habits. Trotsky and Cannon, for instance, were quite different in personality.

In Coyoacán, I saw how Trotsky and Cannon collaborated, and I know what value Trotsky placed on Cannon's opinions as a political strategist and practitioner of Leninism in party building.

As for Cannon, he regarded Trotsky to be a genius, one of the rare individuals like Karl Marx that are born, sometimes generations apart. He accepted Trotsky's genius as a fact, a fact of enormous importance to the revolutionary movement, and he had no thought of placing himself on the same level.

But Cannon never accepted anything on faith from Trotsky, nor would Trotsky have expected it. If Cannon disagreed, he argued for his own views, and on certain questions he convinced Trotsky. Cannon was not unique in this. It was an experience shared by others on Trotsky's staff.

Fourth International

In founding the Fourth International in 1938, Trotsky and Cannon made a powerful combination, beginning with the conversations concerning the program to be presented at the first congress, and ending with the actual launching of the new international party.

There were a number of persons, it should be recalled, even in the Trotskyist movement, who opposed forming the Fourth International, holding it to be inopportune. Both Trotsky and Cannon favored the step, the imminence of World War II making it all the more necessary because of the turbulent new stage in world affairs that would be opened up.

When Trotsky was assassinated in 1940, it was the opinion of many, above all the Stalinists and the reactionaries in general, that this meant the end of the Fourth International and of Trotskyism.

Cannon, at the age of fifty, was considered to be the most prominent leader of the world Trotskyist movement. In his opinion it was unrealistic to believe that any single individual could fill the void left by the death of Trotsky. Most certainly no one should look to him to attempt it. He was no genius, he said, and he considered it pretentious and a mockery to play the role of being one.

However, he did have a plan for carrying on the struggle in the absence of Trotsky. The plan was not an elaborate one. It consisted of closing ranks, of trying to keep the team together, of strengthening it, of expanding it, and of renewing it.

In this way the continuity of leadership could be maintained. If another Trotsky appeared, that would be extraordinary good luck. It would help shorten the struggle for socialism. But if another Trotsky did not appear, we would continue to struggle on the basis of Trotsky's program and teachings, and eventually teamwork would win.

In this proposed course, Cannon considered the Fourth International to be of central importance. Everything possible had to be done to maintain the Fourth International and to expand it on all continents as a means of upholding the program of Trotskyism and of helping to form national leaderships capable of building mass parties and of guiding revolutionary struggles to success.

Cannon's interest in the development and welfare of the Fourth International had nothing in common with a federalist concept that viewed the international as being a good thing so long as it stayed out of the bailiwick of the Socialist Workers Party, as some have claimed.

Cannon was deeply committed to building the Fourth International along the lines laid down at its foundation. He considered the Socialist Workers Party to be only a section of the Fourth International—an important section in his opinion. He never changed in this, even though the passage of reactionary legislation in the United States compelled the Socialist Workers Party to disaffiliate from the Fourth International.

Greatest achievement

Comrade Cannon's most remarkable achievement, nonetheless, was on American soil. Sharing in this achievement were the other pioneer Trotskyists in the United States—among them Vincent R. Dunne, Carl Skoglund, Arne Swabeck, and above all Rose Karsner, Jim's companion who died in March 1968. These pioneer Trotskyists, however, would all give the main credit to Jim.

This achievement was to build a viable nucleus of a revolutionary party inside the United States, the main bastion of world capitalism. Not only did Jim build this nucleus, he maintained it and continued to build it for an unprecedented number of decades in face of enormous pressures. There has been nothing like it in the history of the revolutionary socialist movement.

Jim held this nucleus together against the lure of posts in the trade union bureaucracy, none of which are without considerable emoluments.

He held this nucleus together against the merciless blows and venomous slanders of American Stalinism, once a powerful force in the radical movement and in many trade unions in the United States.

He held this nucleus together in face of the hysteria of World War II, marching to prison at the head of the Trotskyists convicted as the first victims of the Smith Act for their political opposition to imperialist war.

He held this nucleus together during the infamous decade of McCarthyism in the United States, when the Trotskyists were hounded from their jobs by the American political police, the FBI, and when our movement was almost completely isolated politically and virtually paralyzed for lack of funds.

He held this nucleus together against the deadly combination of McCarthyite repression and economic prosperity that led to years of passivity in the labor movement.

Casualties

There were casualties, of course. Valuable comrades grew discouraged and dropped out of activity. Cadres with years of experience could not endure the strain and developed political differences that gave them seeming justification for finding a road to the sidelines.

But new recruits replaced them. And some of these recruits proved to be of exceptional worth precisely because they swam against the stream in joining the movement in such a period.

Jim's stamina and stubbornness won out in the end. He succeeded in maintaining the continuity of leadership. This continuity went back directly to the founders of American socialism in the past century, and back in a direct line to the Bolsheviks, and through them to the founders of scientific socialism.

The nucleus of revolutionary socialists assembled, maintained, and renewed under the leadership of James P. Cannon is doing quite well today and we know of the satisfaction he found in this success.

Development of cadres

During his years as the main leader of American Trotskyism, Jim became the teacher of three, if not four, generations of revolutionists. He taught us not so much through formal lectures—he did not give many in reality—or even through his writings, although here he left us a considerable legacy.

He taught us most powerfully through participating with us in struggles. Over the years he stood at our side in many situations and battles in the class struggle, where one of his chief concerns was the development of cadres, particularly the capacity of comrades to think for themselves.

But I would say that the primary arena in which Jim taught us the most important lessons was in the development of the Socialist Workers Party itself. Here I think not only of party administration, the organization of branch work, the production of our press, and the development of leadership abilities in these areas, but of the many internal struggles, including those in the early years of the Communist Party in which most of us here did not participate except vicariously through the accounts that have been handed down.

Our party owes its very existence to the way Jim handled these struggles. Through them he imparted his political know-how so that it became an acquisition of the cadres as a whole, something our party can use as a foundation in the mighty struggles lying ahead that will determine the fate of America and along with America the fate of the world.

In the aftermath of World War II, it was Jim's firm opinion that the victory of the Soviet Union, the toppling of capitalism in Eastern Europe, and the revolutionary victory in China would ultimately weaken Stalinism on a world scale, making possible new revolutionary advances. The victory of the Cuban revolution in 1959 was one of the confirmations, in his view.

His eyes were set, of course, on the American workers. In the long run, the upheavals elsewhere would have a cumulative effect in the political arena in the United States. Coupled with the ever-deepening economic and social contradictions of capitalism, the American workers, the mightiest power on earth, would be propelled into action and the American revolution would begin.

In the last years of his life, Jim was convinced that the American revolution is not far off. It has drawn perceptibly nearer. He saw the signs in the appearance of the Black liberation movement in the sixties and the women's liberation movement in the early seventies. He saw it in the incapacity of American imperialism to win outright victories, first in Korea and then in Vietnam. He saw it in the radicalization of the youth on a scale never before seen in America. He saw it in the antiwar movement that swept this country from coast to coast, shaking the capitalist political system so that one president decided not to run for a second term, and his successor—a less astute crook—had to hand in his resignation, the first time that has happened in American history.

All these signs led Cannon to believe that the time of Trotskyism is close at hand.

In his personal life, Jim preferred a simple existence, in the company of congenial comrades and friends. He was an omnivorous reader, but he also enjoyed conversation. His conversation, of course, centered on politics, or drifted there, sometimes with a little ribbing and joking woven in.

Jim smoked cigars and a pipe and was not at all demanding as to the grade of tobacco, smoking with equal relish the cheap brands he bought and the Havanas or mixtures that came as gifts in recent years. So long as the tobacco smoldered, he was satisfied.

He considered a celebration from time to time to be a necessity and he made sure that the usual source of conviviality was not missing. For long periods, his drink was tea or at the most beer, a limitation he did not approve of; but alcohol gave him a problem he was compelled to take into account.

In his working pattern, Jim was not an easygoing type; in fact, he could be very demanding. Some comrades found this to be trying and it led to friction in some instances.

Jim had the capacity to recognize his own faults and weaknesses. To close friends, he even overemphasized them, thinking he had more than the usual share.

Jim's objectivity extended to others. It can be seen in the most striking way in his comments on figures he once knew in the Communist Party who had become Stalinists and betrayed the revolutionary socialist movement. He gave them full credit for what they once were and had sought to be, and explained how forces they did not understand had overwhelmed them.

A team man

A psychoanalytical study of Jim might be of interest, for he was very complex, but it would not tell us much about what made him tick politically. He lived as a political person and he must be judged on that level. In this he functioned as a team man, completely conscious of the power of a leadership team, and a master at constructing one; that is, a well-balanced group composed of contrasting types whether one-sided or many-sided, including some always inclined to be critical and some certain to reflect the opinion of this or that layer.

As an integral part of the team, Jim subordinated himself completely to party discipline, to "duty" as he liked to think of it, or to a call to "pitch for the party."

Jim described himself as at bottom an "anarchist," and no doubt there was some truth to this. It did not come natural to him to be a team man. He had to learn it and to apply it quite consciously to himself, harnessing himself to the call for duty. Consequently, it was observable that he indulged in his anarchistic inclinations, if that's what they were, only in small things, doing his utmost to exclude them from anything of importance to the party.

An angry person

Fundamentally, Jim was an angry person. He was angry at injustice, at inequities, at special privileges, at exploitation. He was angry at poverty, lack of opportunity, oppression, racism, and sexism.

He seethed over the crimes of capitalism, its wars, its reactionary ideologies. He hated its police, its courts, its prisons, its fascism, its tendency to drop back to barbarism.

He burned with fury over Truman's dropping the atomic bomb on Hiroshima and Nagasaki and at the chance that the human race might be obliterated in an atomic holocaust.

This deep-seated and perpetual anger at capitalism, aroused every day by what he read in the papers and saw on all sides, was one of the driving forces in Jim's makeup.

He was utterly dedicated to overthrowing this monstrous system in which we happen to have been born.

Jim had a clear vision of socialism and the perspectives it could open up. He gained this vision as a youth and the vision never left him. He sought throughout his conscious life to impart this vision to others, to inspire them, and to win them to the cause.

He repeated this appeal with all the eloquence at his command in the recent speech he made on tape for the celebration of the tenth anniversary of *Intercontinental Press*.

That speech could be said to be Jim Cannon's last message to the party and to the new generation of rebels, expressing his deepest convictions.

He remains with us

I will not say farewell to Jim. He remains with us. He remains with us through his writings. He remains with us through the party that he did so much to establish. He remains with us through the continuity of that party's leadership and through the personal example he set of lifelong dedication to the cause of the emancipation of humanity.

Through these achievements, Jim will remain a participant, a comrade-in-arms, in the international struggle for socialism until the final victory is won.

KAROLYN KERRY: 'JIM STROVE TO MAKE THE PARTY INTO AN EFFECTIVE INSTRUMENT'

For Karolyn Kerry and Tom Kerry, as with Joe and Reba Hansen, 1974 marked their fortieth year as comrades and co-workers with Cannon. Karolyn Kerry told the meeting about some of their experiences with Jim Cannon and Rose Karsner and the party.

In his introduction Barnes said, "Some of you here know that after Rose and Jim went to California for good in the 30s, critics inside the SWP soon dubbed the leadership team in New York the 'Dobbs-Kerry regime.' They meant this as a devastating criticism.

"But we Dobbs-Kerryites grabbed it for ourselves, just like an earlier generation did with the banner of the 'Cannon regime.' Jim said he wasn't surprised when I told him this."

Karolyn Kerry, Barnes noted, "was not only the recipient, as so many were, of Jim's party-building ideas, but she was often one of those responsible for putting them into practice." She has taken on such varied responsibilities as business manager of *The Militant*, SWP branch organizer, SWP campaign manager in New York, and organizer of the Civil Rights Defense Committee, which defended the trade unionists and SWP leaders sent to prison during World War II under the Smith Act. Karolyn Kerry now works in the promotion department of Pathfinder Press.

The following are her remarks.

Tom Kerry and I first came to New York as part of the substitute leadership after Jim, Farrell Dobbs, and the other party leaders had been railroaded to prison in 1944 under the Smith "Gag" Act.

We stayed with Rose Karsner, Jim's companion, collaborator, and a long-time party leader in her own right, while Jim was in prison.

Prison regulations required that the "inmates," as they are called, limit their correspondence to members of their immediate families. Rose, therefore, served as the link for Jim's correspondence with the party leadership.

There was one aspect of Jim's correspondence that had Rose and the rest of us completely mystified. When Jim entered prison he was suffering from ulcers. His customary diet was milk and bananas. Under the circumstances, food, as such, was of little interest to him.

When, therefore, his letters began to deal at great length about the most esoteric menus, we were convinced he was attempting to communicate with the party leadership through a code of his own design. Unfortunately, neither Rose nor anyone else in the party leadership had been provided with a key to the code.

Here is a typical example of one menu from the Pathfinder Press book *Letters from Prison* (letter number 30): "This," wrote Jim, "is Sunday morning and I am thinking of a breakfast of soft-boiled eggs with creamery butter, orange juice (iced), milk, crepes suzette and rightly made coffee with cream."

We puzzled greatly over Jim's menus only to learn later that there was no code, and therefore no key, but that Jim, like all the others, was driven to improvising imaginative menus by the spartan diet imposed by the prison authorities.

In fact, a key to the solution to the puzzle was provided in letter number 125—ninety-five letters later—which reads: "You can tell the friends who inquire about my health that I am all right. I continue to stick strictly to my diet of boiled eggs and milk three times a day, seven days a week, and will stick to it until January 22. Then I think, I will be entitled to a little variety and *I am beginning to look forward to the special menus previously sent to you.*"

But this subject was only incidental to Jim's *real* concern, his constant preoccupation with problems of party politics, strategy, tactics, and especially education. I recall, for example, several very important areas of party activity, which received their initial impetus from Jim's letters.

Subscription drives

1. The proposal for a mass *Militant* subscription drive to be aimed at new readers. Jim thought he was being optimistic when he projected a tentative quota of 3,000 for a 25-cent six-month sub. I can't remember the exact figure of this subscription drive—our first since the war—but I know it exceeded the 3,000 figure. What I *do* remember, however, is that soon after, in 1945, we were achieving goals of more than 20,000 in our *Militant* subscription campaigns.

This drive to make the *Militant* a paper of mass circulation was aided by the work of our first trailblazer team, composed of Eloise Booth and Rudie Rhodes, who traveled by bus from city to city and state to state, selling *Militant* subs to new readers.

2. Party education. In this area Jim conveyed many new ideas of expanding party education for party members and party leaders. He urged us to apply, in this area of party work, the same Bolshevik spirit that animates all of our party-building activities.

It was through Jim's prodding that the first Trotsky School was organized and continued for a number of years thereafter. In a sense we can justly attribute the past several annual educational conferences of the Young Socialist Alliance and the Socialist Workers Party to his reiterated emphasis on organized and systematic educational activities.

I cannot in these few minutes even begin to summarize all of Jim's thoughts on the ways and means of building the party and making it a more effective instrument of revolutionary struggle.

If there is any generalization I can make about Jim Cannon's character, it was his total commitment, his total immersion, his total concern about the party and with the party, first manifested for me in his letters from prison. That was true of the Jim Cannon I first met in San Francisco in 1934, until the day he died last Wednesday.

Jim Cannon's life as a revolutionary fighter—as a leader of the IWW, as a founder of the American Communist Party, and as a founder and leader of the American Trotskyist movement—will, I am convinced, provide an inspiration and a guide to all members of the SWP and YSA. And to those yet to come, who will dedicate their lives to the task of carrying forward the struggle—to which he contributed his entire adult life—to overthrow this monstrous, outworn, and decaying capitalist system and to establish a new order, the world socialist society.

This is why we will forever love and cherish the memory of our beloved friend, our comrade, and our peerless leader, Jim Cannon.

TRIBUTE TO CANNON FROM PENG SHU-TSE AND CHEN PI-LAN

Peng Shu-tse and Chen Pi-lan, noted Jack Barnes at the meeting, "were Jim Cannon's oldest leading communist comrades-in-arms—for five and a half decades. On the other side of the globe, the struggle of Chen Pi-lan and Peng Shu-tse was politically linked from the beginning with that of Rose and Jim."

Peng Shu-tse and Chen Pi-lan were founders of the Chinese Communist Party and of the world Trotskyist movement.

Barnes pointed out that Cannon and Peng were present in Moscow as delegates at several of the same congresses of the Communist International, although they never met there personally.

The following is the message from Chen Pi-lan and Peng Shu-tse to the Political Tribute to Jim Cannon.

Jim Cannon's revolutionary spirit and political contributions remain with us, above all the forging of a Bolshevik-type revolutionary party—the Socialist Workers Party.

Jim was the founding leader of the Left Opposition in the United States, whose program was based on Trotsky's document, "Criticism of the Draft Program of the Communist International." This document was printed serially in the early *Militant*.

Under Jim's leadership, the publication of *The Militant* influenced and encouraged the Trotskyist movement in other countries. *The Militant* and other publications of the American Trotskyists were the educators and organizers of Trotskyists around the world. This cannot be stressed too much.

The SWP maintained and even developed the Bolshevik concept of democratic centralism and was the example for the world Trotskyist movement.

Together with Trotsky, Cannon launched the struggle against [Max] Shachtman and [James] Burnham's revisionism in 1939 and 1940. Another major contribution—this time led by Jim—took place in 1953–54 when he launched the fight against Pabloite revisionism.

We hope above all that Trotskyists, especially the young Trotskyists, will carry on in the traditional combative spirit of Jim Cannon and will emulate his leadership in the construction of a Bolshevik party. If you younger Trotskyists follow in his footsteps and further develop the ideas and program which he stood for, you will surely lead the working class to its final victory under the banner of Trotskyism.

ANDREW PULLEY: 'JIM WAS ONE OF THE HEROES OF SOCIALIST YOUTH'

In introducing Andrew Pulley, national chairman of the Young Socialist Alliance, Barnes noted that the YSA leader's presence confirmed a prediction that Jim Cannon had made some 30 years ago. "In one of his letters from prison," Barnes recalled, "Jim talks about the role of the army in radicalizing proletarian youth in certain periods, and he explains how the prisons become schools for revolutionists."

"This was years before Malcolm X, and Attica, and Fort Jackson," he continued.

Andrew Pulley became a socialist in 1969 at Fort Jackson, after he and other GIs had waged a fight for the right to organize discussions of the Vietnam war and racism in the army. He was thrown into the stockade for insisting on the right of GIs to freedom of speech and assembly.

Barnes introduced Pulley as "one of the leading graduates of the Fort Jackson stockade, one of those schools for revolutionists." The following are his remarks.

Jim Cannon was too old to formally join the Young Socialist Alliance, according to our constitution. But we didn't let that stop us.

He was over eighty in years. But in his optimism in the socialist future and his determination to realize it, and in his sense of humor, he was as young as any of us in the YSA.

Jim was like a member of the YSA. He was our senior consultant. Whenever YSA leaders would visit Los Angeles we would meet with him. His door was always open to the YSA.

It is only natural to be a little nervous when you first meet a person of Jim's stature. But as soon as he began to speak, he would relax you. I was amazed, in one of the meetings I had with Jim, at his familiarity with the work of the party and the YSA, his deep interest in the YSA, and his sharp perception of the events of the class struggle, the youth radicalization, and the general political reality of the day.

Jim Cannon appreciated the YSA as a Leninist youth organization. In one of his last interviews, printed in the July–August *Young Socialist*, Jim stated, "The Young Socialist Alliance of today is an entirely new phenomenon, as far as my experience can judge, by its composition, its general activity, and in practically every other way."

Jim was a big partisan of founding the YSA. He felt the YSA had an important role to play on the campuses, in the high schools, and among the youth in general: to lead young people in struggle to change society, and to train young revolutionists for membership in the revolutionary party.

In a speech presented to the West Coast Vacation School in 1964 titled "What It Means to Be a Young Revolutionist Today"—a speech that recruited to the socialist movement a number of people sitting here tonight—Jim spoke of the danger of nuclear annihilation and said: "So we have come to the conclusion that time is shorter. When you join a socialist movement now, you're joining the battle which in your own lifetime—not that of your children, not that of your grandchildren, but in your own lifetime—and even before you reach an advanced age, is going to be settled.

"You have got to be the vanguard of the people who are going to settle it. So being a socialist becomes the central purpose of your life and your activity."

You know, Jim was a YSAer when he was young. They just didn't call it that then. Jim joined the fight for socialism while in high school. One of his first activities was in the defense campaign against the frame-up of Haywood, Pettibone, and Moyer.

As a youth Jim was a footloose rebel. He became

a socialist and spread the socialist word, speaking on street corners and selling the *Appeal to Reason,* the popular socialist weekly. That was almost seventy years ago. He stayed with that fight for way over half a century, and that's a *long* time.

How many of you have been told, by your parents, teachers, bosses, parole officers, or lieutenants, that you'll outgrow your socialist views when you grow up and get wise?

Well, Jim Cannon grew up, and he *did* get wiser—and that's why he stayed true to his rebel ideas *all the way.* As he explained in the recent *Young Socialist* interview, "If I can convey any suggestion to you it's this—the longer you live in this fight, the more determined you are to try to win it and the more confident you are that the human race will survive."

In one of his letters written from Sandstone federal prison in Minnesota in 1945 Jim wrote, "The young relate the word to the deed. They are moved and inspired by *example.* That is why they demand *heroes;* nobody can talk them out of it."

Those words could not be truer. The Young Socialist Alliance has found the greatest inspiration in the example set by Jim Cannon, one of its heroes.

PEGGY BRUNDY: 'HE WAS AN ACTIVE PARTY MEMBER AND EDUCATOR TO THE END'

In introducing Peggy Brundy, Jack Barnes first explained how Cannon's work had been organized in his last years.

"Rose Karsner and Jim Cannon set up shop on Hyperion Avenue soon after they arrived in Los Angeles," he said, "and after Rose's death (in 1968) Jim christened the house 'the Hyperion commune.' That's because the party always had a team of comrades living there with Jim. They shared the chores; they shared the education in the house; and they shared the mischief that Jim would every so often start up."

"In addition," Barnes continued, "there was always one comrade assigned to organize the whole setup and to expedite the production of more and more of Jim's books as resources permitted. There were five who enjoyed that unique responsibility over the last seven years—Bea Hansen, Peggy Brundy, Andrea Morell, Jessica Star, and Suzanne Weiss."

The following are Peggy Brundy's remarks on what the household was like.

Living and working with Jim, we came to know him as a revolutionary leader and as a human being. We also learned a great deal about the party and about politics. This was no accident. Jim worked at it. But his method of educating was very, very different from the pompous, alienating variety found in colleges.

He worked at eliminating all barriers between himself and his comrades. I think we were all awestruck when we first met him. When I was part of the household, comrades meeting him for the first time would sometimes ask me, "How do I address him? 'Comrade Cannon'? Maybe even, 'Mr. Cannon'?" Well, Jim wanted to be called . . . "Jim."

Education, for Jim, was a give-and-take situation, whether he was talking with a leading cadre of the party or a brand-new recruit. Anyone who worked with Jim became part of his team.

He outlined this approach toward education in a letter he wrote while he was working on his book *Letters from Prison*. He wrote: "A prime obligation of a revolutionary leader is to explain the reasons for what he proposes and does, thus enabling the entire movement to participate in his thinking."

This kind of education was an integral part of the household routine. It took place through casual conversations at the dinner table, meetings with visitors, books and papers he urged us to read, and even jokes he told us while we were watching television. It was a continuing process. Jim didn't just give us the right answers. He tried to teach us how he approached problems.

Most of the essential lessons he drew for us are recorded in his books and are available for everyone to read and study. But occasionally he would remember a new incident in the class struggle, or a story about an individual that illustrated an important lesson. He worried about how these unrecorded anecdotes would be preserved for future generations. He sometimes said that our only hope was that the FBI had the house bugged, so that after the revolution we could transcribe the tapes. We plan to do just that.

One of the projects he carried out over the past year and a half was a series of interviews with comrades and friends—conducted largely by Harry Ring—in which he tried to pass on these previously unrecorded incidents.

He eagerly welcomed visitors. This was one of the ways he sought to keep abreast of current developments in the class struggle.

He spent hours reading each day. He studied the internal bulletins and the press of the party, and he followed the capitalist press. He subscribed to the

New York Times Book Review, The Nation, and *New Republic,* as well as the papers of other tendencies. He considered this very important for keeping in touch with what was going on in the world and with how the different classes and political currents were reacting to it.

He was always thinking about ways to improve the party. His concerns ranged widely, from the problems of building the Fourth International to ideas such as the prepaid subscription card to the *Militant.* He carried out all of these activities, and more, in spite of failing health.

Women's rights

Jim was a long-time supporter of women's rights. His first public speech was a debate with another Rosedale, Kansas, high school student on the question, "Should women be allowed to vote?" Jim defended the affirmative—and he won. Over the next seventy years he never changed that position of support.

In an interview he gave just last month, he said, "The party has recruited women comrades on a scale never seen before in the radical movement. Forty percent of our members are women and, I think, about 40 percent of our staff members are women. This takes place not as a quota policy, but just naturally. So many talented women have come forward to fill this or that position."

Most of all, Jim educated us by his example. When I first met him in 1968, he had been a leader of the revolutionary movement for around sixty years. *Letters from Prison* had just been published, a book that passes on to our generation many of the most basic lessons he had to teach about party building. But he was seventy-eight years old. He was deeply shaken by the recent death of Rose Karsner.

By anybody's standards, he could have retired. He had already given the party a tremendous amount. And he could have decided to just sit back and take it easy for the rest of his life.

But he didn't. With the help of those who worked with him, he organized his life so that in his remaining years he could continue functioning as an *active party member*—to the maximum degree that he was able.

That, I think, is the primary legacy of the last years of Jim's life. In spite of personal hardships—and he suffered many during those years—he remained steadfastly true to the principles that had guided him all his life. He remained convinced that there *can* be a better world if we are willing to *fight* for it.

He once said, "I came out of Rosedale, Kansas, forty years ago looking for truth and justice. I'm still looking, and I won't give one percent discount."

Jim Cannon's approach to life and to the party was summed up by Rose Karsner in 1962 in some remarks she made at a banquet celebrating the publication of *The First Ten Years of American Communism.* I'd like to close by quoting from what she said:

"From the moment we threw our lot in with the socialist movement, more than fifty years ago, we have never wavered in our conviction that a socialist world will come into being. Whether we live to see it or not. That's immaterial. We never faltered in our devotion to this conviction, or in our allegiance to the party we believed was working toward that end. In times of personal difficulty, and we all had them, we sometimes took out time to straighten these matters. But never with the idea of dropping out.

"Never did we feel that we were sacrificing for the party. On the contrary, we were always conscious of the fact that to have to give up the party, that would be a sacrifice. Because through activity of the party, we got fulfillment of life and satisfaction and the confidence that we were working not merely for our own little selves, but for the entire human race. We feel the same way tonight. We recommend that way to you all."

Fourth International Hails Cannon's Achievements

The following is the message sent from the elected leadership of the Fourth International and read at the Political Tribute to Jim Cannon.

The death of Jim Cannon is a loss not only to the revolutionary Marxist movement in the United States, but to the world struggle for socialist revolution as well. Throughout his life Cannon embodied the best American traditions of militant class struggle, and combined those traditions with the recognition of the need for constructing the instrument essential for the victory of the proletarian revolution: the Leninist party and the revolutionary international.

He was able to play a crucial role in transforming that theoretical recognition into reality, fighting all his life to build that party in the strongest bastion of world imperialism.

From the IWW to the Socialist Party left wing, from the original American Communist Party to the International Labor Defense and the fight to free class-struggle prisoners like Sacco and Vanzetti, from the struggle in the Communist Party in defense of the Trotskyist program of revolutionary Marxism to the fight for a new party and a new international, from the days of his intimate collaboration with Leon Trotsky and the establishment of the Socialist Workers Party to the decades of activity in building and strengthening that party—Cannon was always guided by the profound conviction that without revolutionary leadership the struggle of the workers for a socialist world would be in vain.

Neither the Palmer raids nor the Smith Act trials, nor the McCarthyite witch-hunt, nor the constant and severe pressure of the American ruling class was able to deter him from acting resolutely on that conviction.

His more than six decades of revolutionary activity stand as an inspiration to the new forces in the world now rallying to the program and banner of the Fourth International. It is an inspiration that is not merely moral but practical as well, offering the richest lessons for the new generation of revolutionary fighters.

We all mourn the loss of this comrade and we pledge ourselves to continue the fight for the program, party, and goals to which Jim dedicated his long and fruitful life.

United Secretariat of the Fourth International

GEORGE NOVACK:
'JIM TAUGHT US WHAT TO DO NEXT—AND THEN GO AHEAD AND DO IT'

The enormous show of revolutionary financial support at the Political Tribute to Jim Cannon was presided over by George Novack. Novack was a collaborator with Cannon in the revolutionary socialist movement for 41 years.

Jack Barnes, chairman of the meeting, noted that, "beginning with their defense of Jim as one of the victims of the Smith Act frame-up, Evelyn Reed and George Novack worked with Jim as comrades, teachers, friends—and even friendly critics once in a while. And they did it in everything from party literary work, to work in defense of civil liberties, to fund raising—conscious preparation and success in the latter being something Jim insisted on."

The following are George Novack's remarks launching the James P. Cannon Party-Building Fund.

Jim Cannon taught us that the imperative of practical revolutionary politics is to know what to do next—and then go ahead and do it. So what must we do after having paid tribute to Jim's achievements and set forth the significance of his career?

In the opinion of the leaderships of the Socialist Workers Party and the Young Socialist Alliance, no more appropriate and urgently needed step can be taken than to launch at this meeting the James P. Cannon Party-Building Fund.

This is a special, once-in-a-lifetime testimonial to which all members and friends may contribute. As the name indicates, the proceeds will be used for whatever is currently required to promote the kind of party he showed us how to create.

Here, too, we can turn to his own example and take a cue from his views on the role of finances in the building of the revolutionary vanguard. These were formed very early in his activity in the class struggle.

As a young rebel, Jim became a volunteer traveling organizer for the IWW. He spoke at many an outdoor rally as an agitator. The Wobbly soapboxers were accustomed to selling literature and taking up a collection for the cause at the end of each meeting. That enabled the organizer to feed himself and get to the next town.

When a respected comrade died in the fight, the Wobblies' attitude was imperishably expressed by Joe Hill's testament: "Don't mourn, organize!"

The slogan of these educational sessions has been "Educate, agitate, organize." The whole week has objectively been a tribute to Jim. And, as its climactic act, the fund will offer to every one of us the opportunity to help continue with the work of "educating, agitating, and organizing" that Jim began 46 years ago—and to do so in his militant and self-fulfilling spirit. I say self-fulfilling rather than self-sacrificing because that's the way he looked at it.

Jim felt that this generation of party builders had succeeded in professionalizing our finances to a degree qualitatively superior to anything known before. He was most interested in hearing reports about an expansion-fund goal or a campaign rally collection, and would often marvel at the results.

One of the secretaries in his house told me that he would recall how in the early "dog days" the whole national office budget of the Trotskyist movement, including the staff, *The Militant*, and our magazine, amounted to no more than $100 a month.

Jim had a revolutionary proletarian attitude toward money, including his own. It was something to be used, not saved up. What little money he and Rose ever had—and it was usually a party subsistence—was at the disposal of the movement. His legacy to us was not in material things, but in ideas and force of example.

Another of his secretaries told me, "I can't think of a single item Jim owned, other than some things of sentimental value. His notion of comfort was a good cigar or pipe, a bright lamp to read by, dinner at six o'clock without fail, and a household of congenial people."

Jim knew that the socialist movement was a poor people's movement and, if it were a true and healthy workers party, that party could rely only on its own members and sympathizers to finance its revolutionary needs.

It happens by coincidence that Jim's death fell on the same day of the year, Aug. 21—and within a couple of hours—as Trotsky's 34 years before. I attended the memorial meeting held in New York City at which Jim delivered his speech "To the Memory of the Old Man," reprinted in the book *Speeches for Socialism.*

In it he answered the question that was uppermost in the minds and hearts of those present: "Will the movement which [Trotsky] created and inspired survive his death? Will his disciples be able to hold their ranks together, will they be able to carry out his testament and realize the emancipation of the oppressed through the victory of the Fourth International?"

"Without the slightest hesitation," Jim declared, "we give an affirmative answer to this question." And the wise leadership he gave our party and the world movement demonstrated that he fulfilled his responsibilities.

Now we, who are Cannon's disciples, are called upon to give an equally affirmative answer. All of us can participate here and now, *to the measure of our means*, in making it possible for the party he fashioned, and the youth he cherished, to move confidently forward and take the next steps in strengthening the party of the coming American socialist revolution.

He wholeheartedly dedicated his conscious life to that glorious goal. I believe I speak the sentiment of us all in saying: We can and we will do no less.

We have not set a specific goal for the fund we are starting tonight. We know very well what the urgent needs of our movement are at this juncture. But we don't know what the will, the capacity, the ways and the means of our cadres actually are. You will have to show us and guide us by your response to this memorable occasion, to this turning point in the evolution of our movement.

INTERNATIONALISM IS THE CENTRAL PRINCIPLE OF OUR ENTIRE MOVEMENT

James P. Cannon delivered the following speech via tape to the tenth anniversary celebration of Intercontinental Press on May 5, 1974.

This celebration of Joe and Reba Hansen's tenth year as the producers of the great international publication *Intercontinental Press*, combined with the celebration of their forty years of active work—and I mean work—in the movement, should make it clear from the start that this movement was not born yesterday.

Then, if we add to these two momentous events the fact that we are also celebrating the forty-sixth year of *The Militant*, it sets the theme for the whole celebration, which might be properly called "Where We Started and Where We Are Going."

We started with the conception, which we learned from Trotsky, that the central principle of all revolutionary activity in this epoch must be the conception of internationalism—as opposed to the nationalist theory of Stalin and his gang of "socialism in one country." We have stuck firmly to this principle throughout all the intervening years. And that is the reason, first of all and above all, why we are still here and still going forward.

On top of all their other work since they joined the movement in 1934, Joe and Reba have been consistent upholders of the principle of internationalism and have promoted this idea, as they promote everything they believe in, by active work for its fulfillment. For that, we honor them above all tonight, and the Tenth Anniversary of *Intercontinental Press* is a good time to say it out loud.

The world we live in is formally divided up into all kinds of countries great and small, but in reality this nationalism is an obsolete idea. In reality, we live on one planet, and all the countries and all parts of it are joined together in mutual interdependence. And what is done by one country affects all the others as the part affects the whole. This requires that they all find a way to work together as one—until eventually they actually all become one single country. Or if you want to express it another way, one single planet, each part contributing its share to the whole, and the whole affecting the lives of each single unit.

The whole system of capitalism, with its exploitation of the many who do the useful and productive work by a very small minority who produce nothing and contribute nothing, has long been obsolete. Just as the division of the world into national states belongs to the past and has no rightful place in the present and will be done away with entirely in the future.

'We believe in socialist future'

We believe in the socialist future and are confident that it will be realized. But this will not happen by itself. The perpetuation of capitalism can lead to nothing but destruction in economic crises, wars, and eventual destruction of the entire human race, if it is allowed to go its own course. But we firmly believe it will not be allowed to do that. The working class of the world, whose power is unlimited, will act in time to avoid such a catastrophe by eliminating capitalism and inaugurating the socialist society of the future.

But even this historical process will not take place automatically. It requires the intervention of those who are conscious of the great historical necessity and are capable of explaining it to others, until a sufficient number of the workers acquire the same consciousness and act accordingly in a socialist revolution.

We begin our movement with the recognition

that internationalism is the central principle of our entire movement, and that internationalism means, first of all and above all, collaboration of those people in all countries who recognize the international character of our historical problem.

International collaboration means that those who understand the historical problem, and agree on the basic principles which must guide the movement towards its solution, must learn how to work together, exchange ideas, think together, learn from each other—and learn how to solve all the problems which arise in the course of historical development by this collaboration of each and every individual in our movement, in all countries and on all continents.

This indispensable collaboration on an international scale will not happen automatically any more than the abolition of capitalism and its replacement by a socialist order will happen automatically. Both require deliberate thought and conscious effort to solve the problems of working together, of collaborating in this great historical task. This holds true also in the present national fields in each and every country. People must learn how to work together and think together so that the work and thought of each individual becomes a contribution to the whole.

The great lessons of the Russian revolution, which marked the historic turning point from capitalism to socialism on a world scale, were accomplished by the collaboration of many people of different abilities, of different talents and different capacities, who had combined their efforts in a revolutionary party. And this party, in turn, supplied the leadership to the working class which alone has the power to make the revolution and transform society.

The two comrades whom we honor tonight are models of this capacity to work together, not only as a team of two but as a part of a larger team in this country and, especially in the last ten years, have made their great contributions to the development of the international movement as models of collaborators and team workers. They have contributed mightily to the dissemination of this idea to comrades around the world through the magnificent publication which they started, and

have continued to publish and reach ever wider circles of readers, *Intercontinental Press.*

Among the many contributions that Joe and Reba have made in national and international collaboration has been the understanding, and the application in practice, of the fundamental idea that every person in the movement is important; and that everyone's contribution, in whatever field it may be, makes up a part of the whole which makes the movement possible.

I believe this celebration tonight will be another contribution to the great idea that everyone's work for the party is important; and as Trotsky expressed it once, that each of us carries on his shoulders a particle of the fate of humanity, and that thereby our lives are not lived in vain.

HOW WE OVERCAME ULTRALEFTISM IN DEFENSE WORK

The following interview with James P. Cannon, the founder of the American Trotskyist movement, was granted to Syd Stapleton October 29, 1973.

The interview begins with a reference to the Political Rights Defense Fund. This is a committee seeking public support for a $27-million suit for damages filed last July 18 by the Socialist Workers party and the Young Socialist Alliance against Nixon and other government officials.

The suit charges that government agencies, including the Federal Bureau of Investigation, carried out illegal wiretapping, mail tampering, job discrimination, and harassment of SWP and YSA members and supporters. It also cites incidents of SWP campaign headquarters being fire-bombed, bombed, and burglarized.

Contributions to help finance the suit can be sent to: Political Rights Defense Fund, 150 Fifth Avenue, Room 737, New York, N. Y. 10011.

QUESTION: What is your opinion of the Political Rights Defense Fund?

ANSWER: It's a proper and correct procedure to exploit every possibility to utilize what cracks there are in the bourgeois-democratic system to advance our ideas. It's like taking part in their elections. It's wise to utilize a situation like this to explain our ideas to a wider audience.

This wasn't known to the old radical movement. The old radical movement tended toward the ultraleft view that courts are crooked instruments of the capitalist class, so why bother? Ignore them. Including the elections. That was the prevailing opinion of the syndicalists and red-socialist wing in which I was.

But I don't blame myself for being an ultraleftist in those days. I didn't know any better and there was nobody to teach us better. The only ones who spoke the other way were the right-wing socialists who thought you could accomplish everything through the ballot box. We were pretty sure that was false.

It was not until after the Russian revolution and Lenin wrote his pamphlet on the infantile sickness, explaining how revolutionists could utilize parliamentary action effectively, that we got straightened out on that. It was so damned simple and so convincing that I don't have any patience with people who still repeat the old arguments of the ultraleft before the Russian revolution.

I can recall instances in the early days where Lenin's approach could have been effective. One was the Lawrence, Massachusetts, textile strike of 1912. That was sixty-one years ago. It was a famous IWW strike. Bill Haywood, Elizabeth Gurley Flynn, Carlo Tresca, Joe Ettor, Arturo Giovannitti were involved in it.

Retrospectively, I recall one incidence that has a bearing on this question of whether you should utilize bourgeois-democratic institutions. At that time Victor Berger was a Socialist congressman from Milwaukee. He was the first Socialist congressman in the United States. But he was a right-winger. He was the leader you might call the ultra-right wing of the Socialist party. Notwithstanding that, the strike leaders were able to use his position to gain tremendous publicity for the strike. They cooked up a wonderful idea for publicity—to take the children of the strikers on the train to socialist sympathizers in various places to be kept during the strike. It caused a great sensation. The Lawrence authorities interfered and tried to put a stop to it. The use of the police created a furor.

Then Victor Berger introduced a resolution in Congress to investigate the Lawrence strike. He got an official committee set up, and Haywood and the leaders brought the kids and women to the congressional hearings to testify about conditions. It was a wonderful publicity job that helped win the strike.

But it was not a normal procedure. Retrospectively I see it as a good example of how to use a bourgeois parliamentary institution.

Another example I recall was in 1917 when the Socialist party came out against the war. Morris Hillquit, in the New York municipal elections that year, ran for mayor and made the war question his main issue. It got tremendous publicity across the country.

I didn't realize it then because I was still a hidebound syndicalist, but I look back on it as a wonderful illustration of how even a municipal campaign can be utilized for a national political purpose.

I really rejoice over the way our party goes into these elections, national, state, and local—any place they can get an edge in and get up some kind of an audience, newspaper space, some TV or radio time, and do it without giving away anything. That's all for free.

I see all these ultrawise, ultraleft groups. What do they do? They stand around with their mouths open while we exploit the cracks and crevices in the bourgeois-democratic system without paying the slightest respect to it. You know, they can't run a bourgeois-democratic system without giving a little opening here and there. So, we take advantage of it; and we're 100 percent right!

Q: In the history of the radical movement has there ever been a crisis in government with the kind of impact that the Nixon-Watergate crisis has had? Why do you think this Nixon thing has developed to the degree it has?

A: That's what Nixon would like to know. There have been some attempts to compare it to the Teapot Dome scandal of the Harding administration. But that was a pure-and-simple graft scandal involving cabinet members and some oil companies. Public sentiment was rather "So what? Don't they all steal?"

The Communist party ran its first presidential candidates in 1924. Foster and Gitlow were the candidates. It was only a token campaign; but one of the slogans we started out with was "Down with the Capitalist Teapot Dome! Vote for Communist candidates for president."

Our comrades were somewhat taken aback by the reception to that. People would say, "You mean to tell us that if your guy got in there he wouldn't steal? All politicians steal." There was absolute cynicism, more or less indifference. "What the hell; so they stole a few million dollars."

I think that would have been the attitude now if Watergate had been limited to graft. What's involved in this case is the extent of the bugging, espionage, and intimidation. A large section of the population, including a large section of the middle and upper classes, got apprehensive about it.

It's not the same as the Teapot Dome scandal. There is a genuine public reaction to this scandal. You might say, multiple scandal. Every day, you expect something new to be revealed.

A columnist named Kraft. Do you know him?

Q: Joseph Kraft. He's the fellow who went to Paris and was followed by the CIA, I believe.

A: He's a prominent national columnist. He wrote an article summarizing the whole thing in one of the liberal magazines. His opinion was that this Nixon outfit and the hatchetmen he had around him were actually moving in the direction of a police state. The ruling powers in this country don't think they need that yet. The opposition comes, you know, not only from the workers. It comes from practically all circles of society. The *New York Times* and the *Washington Post* and the *Los Angeles Times* are all hostile to this administration. They represent real money in this country. If there is a conflict in the upper circles, the difference between the old money and the new may be involved, I think. The new tycoons don't know where to stop; they haven't learned moderation, or the need for concessions. The older ones think it's better to give a little in order to keep a lot.

Q: When the International Labor Defense had to fight cases like Sacco-Vanzetti and Mooney-Billings, was it able to take advantage of any divisions like that in the ruling class over how to react to the labor movement? Was it able to build up support for its cases through both mass propaganda work and things like endorsements?

A: Yes, there were many endorsements and they were utilized. Even lawyers were outraged at the violations of the rules of law. The Sacco and Van-

Left to Right: James P. Cannon, Felix Morrow, and Albert Goldman

zetti case was a frame-up. Everybody knew it was a damned frame-up from beginning to end.

The witch-hunt began in the early 1920s. There was a tremendous red scare and they arrested thousands of people overnight in the Palmer raids. They deported whole shiploads of immigrants who were suspected of subversion or of being connected in any way with the radical movement. They just hit on Sacco and Vanzetti in the course of a general investigation. They had no case against them at all. They framed it.

The judge was outspokenly prejudicial in all his rulings and so on. They went through with it. It was delayed by one appeal after another and by public protest for seven years. It was not till 1927 that they finally executed them. And there were deep feelings in the movement of protest.

A couple of years ago a book was published that tried to justify the killing of Sacco and Vanzetti. The author tried to prove that Carlo Tresca had stated in one instance that while one of them was innocent the other was guilty. And since Carlo Tresca was a prominent anarchist, he thought that this was big news. He said also that I knew about it—that I thought they were guilty despite the fact that I was organizing the campaign of the International Labor Defense. He made these statements in *The New Republic.*

I immediately wrote a reply which they published under the heading "What Cannon Didn't Think."

Judge Musmano, who had been connected with the Sacco-Vanzetti Committee, and later became a prominent judge in Pennsylvania, wrote me a very, very warm letter congratulating me on my protest in *The New Republic.* Which is an indication he still had strong convictions about the case although he was by no means sympathetic to anarchism or any other radical idea.

Q: As a result of the tapes controversy and the whole development of this struggle around Nixon's role in Watergate, there's quite a bit of sentiment in various circles, from George Meany to radical students, to impeach Nixon. As far as I know, that's a totally new phenomenon. Do you have any opinion about how revolutionists should relate to demands for impeachment?

A: The only other case involved was that of President Johnson, who succeeded Lincoln. That was in 1866, over a hundred years ago. No, there has been nothing like the exposure of the Nixon administration.

He's committed to something that's unforgiveable in the eyes of the moneyed rulers of this country. He's gone too far; he's stirred up too much trouble. They want to rule the country rather calmly. They're getting plenty of benefits the way it's working. They're not ready to use police-state methods to the extent Nixon has used them.

And then there's been some bad luck. One thing leads to another. A witness incidentally mentions to the Ervin Committee that they kept tape recordings of all the conversations. My god, is that so? Accidental things like that led from one revelation to the next.

I think our press is doing all right in covering Watergate and should keep hammering away on it from our own special viewpoint that this is just an unusually flagrant example of what capitalist rule and politics are really like.

We should watch out for oversimplification. Some issues of *The Militant* may have given the impression that it was being treated like another Teapot Dome scandal, "Well, they all do it; don't they?"

But Watergate goes beyond anything previous. Even Supreme Court Justice Douglas says he suspects they tapped the Supreme Court, and Johnson suspected that his phone was tapped.

If the ruling class thought all this was necessary, they would be for it, but at present they're not for such extensive use of police-state methods. So I think we should recognize this, and without making any concessions in principle, deal more fully with the way Nixon has embarrassed the real rulers of America.

But, as I say, that's marginal. It's not a fundamental criticism of our handling of the case. I think *The Militant* is doing very well, harping on it all they can, speaking about it all they can.

This morning I received a copy of the *Workers Vanguard*.

Q: That's Robertson's paper.

A: Do you know what they say on the headline? "Impeachment is not enough!" (Laughs.)

Q: He has to be hanged by the thumbs, or something?

A: (Laughs.) Returning to what the attitude of the radical movement used to be toward utilizing the judicial and parliamentary system for revolutionary purposes. Our actions used to be purely defensive. Even in the Sacco-Vanzetti case we took a defensive position. The same was true of the Mooney case and going all the way back to the Haymarket martyrs. They were all defensive actions.

The tendency was to say the courts are crooked, influenced by the capitalist class, and so keep away from them. For instance, the idea of utilizing the courts was not known to me. I recall distinctly in the terrible persecution of the IWW during the First World War. They arrested active Wobblies wherever they could find them. They had so many they put whole groups on trial. Around eighty to one hundred were tried in Chicago. There was another big group in Sacramento, California, and another in Kansas City, Kansas, the Witchita Case, they called it.

This gives you an idea of the decentralization of the IWW and the ultraleft approach to the question of utilizing the courts. In the Chicago and Kansas cases they put up a legal defense with lawyers. But in Sacramento they adopted the policy of a "silent defense." Did you ever hear of that?

Q: Where they refused to speak?

A: A silent defense. They didn't have any lawyers; they used no witnesses; they didn't use cross-examination. They ignored the court. They just sat there. Just to show their contempt.

They got stiff sentences like the others, but all they accomplished by their silent defense and their refusal to employ any lawyers was to lose the possibility of appealing, getting some of their people out on bail while the appeals were pending, and organizing an effective campaign. It was a negative action. It represented the prevailing attitude of the left-wing movement that you couldn't get anything out of the courts.

Now, our policy today is different. We base ourselves on the fact that it's not a police state, it's a bourgeois-democratic state, which a lot of people think is really democratic. In order to maintain that illusion the ruling class has to give you a little leeway here and there.

The intelligent thing, as Lenin explained in his pamphlet on the infantile sickness, is that we utilize these crevices for our own purposes. The suit filed by our party in the Watergate case is a very correct tactic, a serious move to exploit the bourgeois-democratic system in an offensive action in the courts. It's correctness is self-evident when you look at it.

I noticed the New York papers carried reports of the press conference about the filing of the suit. You're going around the country speaking to audiences who wouldn't be there if this issue didn't appeal to them the way it does.

And what are ultralefts doing? Doing nothing except occasionally yapping at us.

Of course we should explain in our general propaganda that we don't expect to get much justice from the capitalist courts. The whole thing is rigged against us. But in order to maintain some illusion of democracy they've got to show some respect for law and order, so we'll take advantage of that and we'll test it out.

The Kutcher case is a wonderful example of how sometimes such a course can be successful.

Q: Why do you think there was such a big difference between the outcome of the Kutcher case and the outcome of the Smith Act trials of the leaders of the Communist party during the same period?

A: Well, the Smith Act trials began with our being tried in Minneapolis. All of these trials were, from the point of view of the letter of the law, illegal and unconstitutional. We were convicted of expressing certain opinions. We were not accused of any actions. The same held true for the Communist party defendants. The political climate—the war, and later the cold war—made it possible for them to get away with it. And they did. But there aren't any Smith Act cases today, are there?

Q: No.

A: We appealed to the Supreme Court. We kept out of jail for two years after our conviction with one appeal after another and the final decision was no decision at all. The Supreme Court refused to

Cannon and Rose Karsner.

hear the case. Did you know that? So it left undecided whether the law was unconstitutional. Later they finally agreed to hear another case and threw out a large section of it. You don't hear a lot about the Smith Act trials any more.

Q: Well, the question that I was raising, the reason I posed it in relation to the Communist party, is that it seems to me that because of the SWP's position of political opposition to the war, there was a clear, nearly unanimous sentiment on the part of the capitalist class that the SWP should be prevented from expressing that point of view. But later, during the witch-hunt, Jimmy Kutcher, a member of the SWP, gained enough support to win, while members of the CP like the Rosenbergs and the Smith Act defendants were virtually isolated. Obviously the question of their relationship to the Soviet Union during the cold-war period of "containing Communism" had something to do with it, but I wondered if there were other questions involved.

A: I don't give the ruling class credit for unanimity of opinion in everything they do. Different judges act in different ways, and the Communist party was particularly unpopular during the cold war because of their connection with the Soviet Union. The witch-hunters thought they could get away with it because of the political climate, and they did.

We're not fighting this case, I hope, with the idea that we're going to get justice. We're fighting to see if we can get a little something out of the pretense of a democratic society. If they make things absolutely airtight, and there's no chance to win any kind of a legal process and so on, then they can't make a pretense of having a democratic order. There's a great distinction between a police state and a bourgeois-democratic system. One has loopholes in it and the other is airtight, until it's overthrown.

Q: Some ultralefts have argued that it's ridiculous for socialists to try to defend legal rights that they have formally under a bourgeois government. We touched on some of those questions before in terms of the Sacramento trial of the IWW. But there are a lot of parallels between this argument and

Max Eastman, James P. Cannon, and William D. Haywood in Moscow in 1922.

the kind of argument that it seems to me Grandizo Munis was presenting in his criticisms of your conduct in the Smith Act trial and so I wonder if you have any comment on whether or not his criticism and your answer would have any relevance to legal actions like the SWP suit today. You were making the point that there is some necessity for the ruling class to grant some democratic rights.

A: They had to grant us a trial which they wouldn't have had to do under a police state. And taking advantage of that, we used the courtroom for a forum. To do that effectively, we conducted a very prudent, dignified defense. We had our own lawyer, Albert Goldman, who was a member of the movement and on trial himself. We worked out together the questions he would ask and answers we would give. And in general we exploited the trial to the full for propaganda purposes.

I thought the Communist party made a mess of their big case in New York by engaging in so many squabbles with the judge on technicalities. The public became impatient and that hurt the defendants.

In contrast to that, our idea was just to get all the propaganda advantage possible out of the case. I don't know how long I was on the stand. Enough to make a small book. All those questions that Goldman put to me—these had all been worked out in advance. And, as far as I can remember, we didn't concede a damned thing to them. We just denied that what we were doing was illegal.

We used defensive formulas. We didn't go in there and shout for the right to use violence or anything like that. We just said the workers have a right to defend themselves and do such things as form a workers defense guard in the Minneapolis strikes.

When the prosecutor kept prodding me on it, and I kept answering defensively, I finally ended, "I think the workers have a right to defend themselves. And if that's treason, you can make the most of it!" I stood up and shouted that at them.

And the whole goddamn courtroom was stunned and he just said, "That's well spoken," and stopped.

When he questioned me about the Russian revolution, he was flabbergasted by my contention that it was a legal act. "What the devil are you talking about?" He didn't say that, but put it in lawyer's language.

I gave some more calculated arguments about revolutions and their legality, and finally said, "I don't think you'll find a more legal revolution than that!"

He said, "That's all." He just threw up his hands. "That's all."

The pamphlet we made of that testimony has been the most circulated of all our publications. I've been told many times that it's most effective in talking with new contacts: *Socialism on Trial.*

Q: I think it's being reissued along with the debate with Munis.

A: Yes, I've heard that.

Q: I have one other question. We've had a lot of experience with defense committees like the one we've set up in this case, the Political Rights Defense Fund. I'd like to know more about the ILD. How did that idea develop? Did it come from some earlier experience in the radical movement in the United States, or was it from international experience?

A: You might say it came about by accident. There was a tradition in America of solidarity in defense cases. The IWW had a defense committee called the General Defense Committee. It was strictly an IWW committee.

Going back to the Haywood case, where I first became involved in the movement as a 16-year-old kid in 1906. The Socialist party in those days was pretty strong and growing, and *The Appeal to Reason*, the socialist paper, with half a million circulation, made the Haywood trial the weekly front-page event.

Then—I don't know where it originated but it proliferated all over the country—Moyer-Haywood conferences were held of delegated bodies of the Socialist party, sympathetic trade unions, Workmen Circles, and so on. Meetings and demonstrations were organized for the defense of Haywood.

He was made candidate for the governor of Colorado while he was on trial. That was a very good stunt.

They employed the best lawyers. Clarence Darrow headed the defense. He was big news himself, he was so famous. The central national defense was controlled by the union because they had to collect a lot of money.

The general procedure was that when someone was arrested, his own organization would set up a defense committee. They'd ask for the support of others, but they didn't broaden out the defense committee. The Sacco-Vanzetti defense committee, in fact, was a little group of Boston anarchists, who kept tight control of everything. The campaign didn't get under way until the International Labor Defense came in on the propaganda side. We didn't participate on the legal and financial side.

In the early twenties, after the uprisings that followed the Russian revolution, the Russian party first set up an organization of their own in Russia to collect funds and so on for the victims of the white terror in Eastern Europe.

In early 1925, when we were there to attend a plenum, a proposal was made to organize international support for the victims of the white terror. The organization was to be called the International Red Aid. It's primary function would be to collect funds and to protest on behalf of the victims of the white terror.

We talked about this in our delegation. We had the custom of congregating in Bill Haywood's room in the Hotel Lux. Bill Haywood and I were talking about it one day, and we came up with, "By God, we ought to do something about the American prisoners." There were a lot of them. There were over a hundred men still in jail from the old prosecution, and new criminal-syndicalist prosecutions were under way in various states. "We ought to do something about the Americans. We ought to broaden this thing out and make the committee take responsibility for the American prisoners—really Americanize the American section."

The more we talked about it, the more the idea took hold. I was then a member of the Political Committee of the Communist party and all I had in mind was just to promote the idea. Get it accepted in Moscow and then, when we came back, have the PC endorse it, take the initiative, get hold of somebody, and do it.

Well, when we got back, I went before the Political Committee for the first meeting, explained what had developed in Moscow, what the proposal was. The fact is that while we were in Moscow, they had sent delegates to the different countries to promote the International Red Aid idea. Their representative here had presented a formal motion that the PC support it. International Red Aid membership cards had already been printed. A very quiet, inoffensive operation—they were going to organize a few committees, get a few dollars for the victims, and let it go at that.

Well, my idea was to expand the operation and make something out of it. The committee immediately adopted my plan. "My idea," I said, "is not only just to have party members. Let's go out and get some prominent people to support it."

There was a defense committee in Pittsburgh on a special case there. There was a defense committee in Chicago on some still pending case of the Communist party. Some old Wobblies might become interested because they had friends still in prison.

I got Ralph Chaplin interested. He wasn't active in the IWW but he was sympathetic. And so were two or three other prominent ex-Wobblies. An ex-Wobbly was not somebody who had repudiated the movement, but somebody who had simply dropped out for personal reasons. They were well-known people. We made them members of the Executive Committee. And in fact in the Executive Committee, as we laid it out in our plans, the majority would consist of nonmembers of the Communist party, people who were sympathetic to the general idea.

The more we talked about it, the more enthusiasm grew. We finally decided that we wouldn't just proclaim this committee; we would organize a national conference to launch the International Labor Defense. We projected publishing a magazine. As I say, the thing simply got out of hand. I recall one meeting just before the conference was called. We were laying out the plans and came to a point about the secretary of the Chicago Defense Committee possibly being named national secretary. Some Wobbly said, "Uh, uh; you got it all wrong."

"What do you mean?"

"You're going to be secretary. You want us to hustle? Well, we're not going to hustle for some fellow we don't know. We know you and we'll support you."

Then it became evident to everybody that I had gotten so deeply involved in the thing and I was so much better known than any of the other potential candidates that I would have to take over. I had never planned on that at all.

Then Rose Karsner said she would like to come in and run the office. She was the head of another organization called the International Workers Aid, which had originally been called the Friends of Soviet Russia. It was organized during the famine of 1921 and had continued as a fund-raising organization for different countries and different movements in need of financial help, where there were famines and persecution, etc.

Q: So it had a separate office with its own staff?

A: Yes. We were going to set up a national office with a secretary and an office manager. We planned it as a big operation. She would come in and run the office so that I'd be free to travel and organize locals and one thing or another.

So it culminated in a good-sized first national conference of the International Labor Defense. We had the endorsement of a lot of prominent people, including Upton Sinclair. We announced that we were defending all prisoners—what we called class-war prisoners—in connection with labor. And there were quite a bunch of them. There was a large number of IWWs in different cases. Mooney and Billings were in prison. The Centralia fight had resulted in a dozen Wobblies being imprisoned. Then we discovered that in Texas, Cline and Rangel, who had been helping Mexican revolutionists, had been framed up and were serving long sentences. In San Quentin were a lot of people who had been sent up under state criminal-syndicalist laws. Up in Maine there was a case. It added up to about 140 people. We said we will help all of them; we'll raise money to send a monthly stipend of $5 a month to every prisoner for commissary.

A commissary is a place in prison where you can buy a little extra stuff. It's very important. You get the routine meal. But if you have a little money you can buy candy bars, cigarettes, cookies, apples, oranges, and things like that. It makes a big difference.

We would send $5 a month to each prisoner and we would send $25 a month to their families, if they had a family. Then we would plan—without promising definitely—we would plan to raise a Christmas fund to give a bonus of $25 or $50 to every prisoner for Christmas. We would publicize all their cases through our magazine and other media. It was a very enthusiastic national conference.

The plan outlined in the constitution made it a membership organization. Anybody sympathetic to the cause could join. Ten cents a month dues and donate whatever you could and if you had a little extra money, send it in to the national office.

We organized locals all over the country and not only that, we put in full-time district organizers in New York, Chicago, Los Angeles, San Francisco, and places like that—Cleveland. Full-time organizers! They coordinated local branches and stirred up activity. The thing took hold and was quite well received.

In 1925 we started the *Labor Defender.* It was an illustrated monthly magazine. In the magazine, on which Max Shachtman was the editor and worked full time, we decided to revive all the old cases. We told the story of the Haymarket martyrs, and Mooney and Billings. We put out a special edition on the lynching of Frank Little in Butte, Montana. We publicized the Sacco-Vanzetti case and campaigned on other cases. It was the most popular magazine in the radical movement. Sold wider than the party press.

The second national conference was in 1926. Elizabeth Gurley Flynn was brought in. She had been very prominent in the IWW. She became national chairwoman and was sent on a national tour. The third national conference in 1927 was held under the slogan: "Third National Conference of the International Labor Defense, Fortieth Anniversary of the Haymarket Martyrs." Lucy Parsons, the widow of the martyr, was the guest of honor. These things were very effective in stimulating a sense of solidarity in the radical movement.

And throughout all that period we kept up our obligation. We sent $5 a month to every one of the one hundred prisoners regardless of what organization they belonged to; but we didn't send it over the head of their own committee. For example, for members of the IWW, we sent it in a lump sum to their general defense committee to distribute; so that we were not interfering with the work of any of the other committees.

Our work was propaganda and agitation, and legal defense only if it was needed. New cases were brought to us and we had quite a number of those. Our Christmas fund was very popular.

YOUTH AND THE SOCIALIST MOVEMENT

Rich Finkel, National Secretary of the Young Socialist Alliance, had the following discussion with James P. Cannon on March 15, 1974, in Los Angeles.

FINKEL: On my tour this spring, I've already visited Texas, Arizona and part of California. I get the impression that many students who were active during the height of the antiwar movement and the Black struggle haven't quite figured out what kind of role they can play in a period of different dimensions, opportunities and problems, such as we are facing right now.

CANNON: I think it's very important for us to adopt a completely realistic view of the situation and adjust to the changed consciousness and attitude on the campus. The party is tested just as much by times like this as by times of an upswing in activity.

During the fifties, we lived so long in hard times, I think some of the old-timers found it difficult to adjust to the big upsurge we had during the Vietnam war.

It should be made a point of our educational propaganda that a revolutionist's spirit and attitude is not determined by the popular mood of the moment. We have a historical view and we don't allow the movement to fade away when it runs into changed times, which can happen as we know from experience.

You're acquainted with my pamphlet, *America's Road to Socialism*? It's a series of six lectures given at the height of the McCarthyite period in the fall of 1952, when reaction seemed to reign supreme. There were practically no actions of any kind. So we decided on the lectures as a deliberate party action. They were given here in Los Angeles as a series of forums on what socialism means. What socialist America will look like. We had a regular attendance of 100, give or take a few, at each lecture.

Don't you find that the young people you talk to have a great interest in what socialism is, what it will look like and so on? There's a temptation in a period of upswing of activities to neglect the exposition of our fundamental program in its historical perspective. But I can recall from my youth, which was in the heyday of the Socialist Party[1] in this country—the Debs[2] period—that seemed to be the question that most interested people who were contacted around the party. What is this socialism? What will it look like? How will it come about? And so on. And I think that's true today too, if you really probe the minds of young people.

FINKEL: We've noticed that quite a bit. I think one of the stimulants right now is the energy crisis. People know that the oil monopolies prevail. They see what capitalism does, and they ask, "What is socialism? How do we organize it? How do we get there?"

We get more of these questions about socialism

1. **Socialist Party.** Prior to World War I the Socialist Party was the major political party of the American socialist movement. After the Russian revolution, the majority of the left wing of the SP was expelled and formed the initial ranks of the Communist Party. With the exception of a brief revival in the thirties, the Socialist Party has continued since World War I to decline in size and influence.

2. **Eugene Victor Debs.** Debs was a great leader of the American labor movement. Between 1900 and 1920 he ran for president of the United States during five elections as the Socialist Party candidate—running in 1920 from a jail cell where he had been imprisoned for his antiwar views and activities during World War I. Although Debs was a leader of the left wing of the SP and a supporter of the Russian revolution, he did not join the young American Communist Party in the twenties. Debs died in 1926.

today than we did during the antiwar movement. I think that the questions are different at this particular period—more fundamental. With the Watergate revelations, people want to know, "How can we organize government without corruption? Is it possible?"

Your pamphlet, *America's Road to Socialism*, was one of the first things I read when I joined the YSA in 1968. It was an old copy, but it answered a lot of questions I had. I think that's true for many YSA members.

Could you explain a little about some of the previous experiences of the workers movement with youth groups? That's one of the questions that we often get in the YSA. What happened with the Wobblies[3]? How did the Socialist and Communist parties build their youth organizations? What were their problems and successes?

CANNON: First of all, we've got to understand that the past of the radical and revolutionary movement in this country is part of our heritage—both with its positive and negative sides. We have to know about that. Our new members should be thoroughly schooled in our exposition and analysis of the preceding movements—their strong points and their errors which we are trying to correct as a result of experience and greater knowledge that we've gained from other sources, most importantly from the Russian revolution.

FINKEL: Did young people play a special role in the Wobblies or in the early Socialist Party? Were there student members? What sort of role did the radicalizing youth find in the socialist movement?

CANNON: The IWW itself was predominantly a young workers movement. It had no special youth organization. The drive and idealism of youth were a large part of its power and its merit, but again, it had no separate youth organization. There was no need for it as far as anybody could see. There was not even any talk of it.

In the West particularly, the IWW was predominantly a movement of migratory workers. They had to be young because it was a hard life. In the Midwest, for example, the harvest would start early in Texas and Oklahoma, and a great mass of migratory workers traveled by freight train down to the centers where the hiring took place and worked a few weeks or a month—whatever it took to finish the harvest.

Then they rode north by freight until they ended up in Minnesota and the Dakotas. That would be the whole summer long. And there would be railroad construction work and things of that kind. Migratory workers, as they were called, were something like the harvest pickers of today, except that they were all single men in those days. The wheat fields of Texas and Oklahoma would just be harvested about the time it was getting ripe in Kansas, and then in Nebraska and so on.

Another big source of their membership was the lumber woods of the Northwest. That constituency consisted of the same type of workers. And in the East in the textile mills, the IWW at one time had a strong movement, many strikes, mostly of young foreign-born and women workers.

Socialist youth organizations

FINKEL: What were the first socialist youth organizations in this country?

CANNON: Well, to my recollection, there have been several histories written of the socialist movement which I think I mentioned in my book, *The First Ten Years of American Communism*. Up until the thirties, the socialist movement didn't amount to much on the campuses. There was a pretty sharp division between students and workers in those days. College boys came from the better off classes and didn't associate with the workers.

The first manifestation of a ripple of the movement on the colleges came when Jack London and Upton Sinclair, who were the two literary heroes of the movement at that time, gave some lectures at

---

3. **Industrial Workers of the World.** Founded in Chicago in 1905, the IWW (also known as the Wobblies) was a workers organization dedicated to the concept of industrial unionism—that is, the concept of organizing workers in large, industry-wide unions, rather than narrow unions according to craft or skill (the policy followed by the American Federation of Labor—AFL).

The IWW stood for the overthrow of the capitalist system, but wrongly believed that an industrial union rather than a revolutionary party could provide the leadership for such a revolutionary transformation of society. For nearly two decades the IWW was the symbol in America of labor militancy and unconditional opposition to the bosses and their schemes. After World War I, the IWW quickly declined in influence.

Yale or Harvard or a place like that on socialism—"How I Became a Socialist" and so on.

They received a favorable response, and the result of it was the formation of what I think was called the Intercollegiate Socialist Society. It was a very thin movement because the percentage of people going to college was not great in those days.

Colleges were by no means the center of radicalization. Just the contrary. They were the center of conservatism. The Intercollegiate Socialist Society, I think, later changed its name to the League for Industrial Democracy (LID). It still exists, doesn't it?

FINKEL: Yes. In fact, SDS—the Students for a Democratic Society—was originally the youth group of LID. Prior to 1959, I think, it was called the Student League for Industrial Democracy. But in 1964 the LID disowned it, because SDS wouldn't exclude groups like the YSA from an antiwar march it was planning in Washington, D.C.

CANNON: Anyway, the Intercollegiate Socialist Society became sort of a gentlemen's socialist club on the campuses. They called it the country club of the movement. The real movement itself had virtually nothing on the campuses. I don't know the exact year when the Young People's Socialist League[4] was formed. You can probably check it in the history books, but it didn't really amount to much before the thirties when there was an upsurge of interest in political questions during the depression. Campus radicalism was at that time dominated by the Communist Party. The Socialists were quite a secondary factor, but they were largely swamped by the Communist Party.

There's been of course a great, fundamental change since then. One of the big changes to note is the percentage of people going to college now. I don't know the statistics, but you can easily check it. I think you'll find that the difference is practically qualitative.

In the old days of the IWW, anybody who'd been to high school was an exception. The average worker was lucky enough to finish grade school, get some kind of job, and that was it. But various factors, including the development of technology and the improved standard of living, greatly expanded the college population. Have you ever thought of that or have you ever read anything about it? Tremendous expansion.

For example, we've had here in our household over the last number of years 15 or 20 people who've lived here with me. There are two people here now. Six months ago there were two others. I think every single one of them had been to college. They were all working. They have either finished college or have had some college experience, but they're working. And I guess a large percentage of those who attend college today go to work not as managers of prosperous family empires, but as workers in the labor force.

In 1919 Harvard students had a great holiday going to Lawrence to help break a strike[5] there. You can hardly imagine such a thing today.

The same thing happened in England in the general strike of 1926. There was a big movement recruiting strikebreakers from universities and prep schools and so on. They tried to help break the general strike.

Student radicalism in the '30s

In the thirties during the depression, that was the first time I ever noticed—the first time it came to general public attention—that there was a great rumbling on campus. The Communist Party had a very strong student membership. The Socialist Party too. We had a few, but nothing numerically significant.

The CP developed an antiwar movement on the campuses during the depression years. They absorbed to a large extent the young socialists, the YPSL people, in a broader movement called the League Against War and Fascism.

The big problem for a person going to college

4. **Young Peoples Socialist League.** YPSL was the youth organization affiliated with the Socialist Party. During the late thirties many of its members were won to Trotskyism. YPSL for a short time (1938–40) broke with the SP to work in cooperation with the Socialist Workers Party. Today YPSL is the youth group of the Social Democrats, USA. YPSL's major current activity has been support to various Democratic Party politicians and to the Zionist state of Israel.

5. **Lawrence Strike of 1919.** Lawrence, Massachusetts, was a major center of textile manufacturing around the turn of the century. In 1919, three months after the end of World War I, a major strike broke out in the textile mills. It lasted three months and was met with vicious repression by local police and hired company goon squads.

then was what you were going to do after you got out. There was no job to go to. That was the fate of many of them.

I remember Ted Draper, the author of *The Roots of American Communism,* told me that he concentrated on the humanities courses in college rather than on the courses that would equip him for some kind of technical job. He said, "What was the use? Everybody knew there was no job to go to." He was preparing himself to be a writer.

An odd little story about the Socialist Party and the Communist Party is the story of the Draper brothers. You've heard of Hal Draper, the perennial YPSL? He's the brother of Ted Draper, the historian. Hal Draper was the Socialist, and the Socialists had a rather militant left wing in those days. He was one of the outstanding leaders of YPSL, and Ted Draper was one of the outstanding leaders of the Stalinists in the New York college community.

I was told that a big feature of that period was the debates between the two Draper brothers over questions of policy, war and so on. Hal Draper was a left-wing Socialist and Ted Draper was a Stalinist. In those days many Socialists stood to the left of the Stalinists.

A great many of those young people recruited by the Stalinists came out of college—either as graduates or dropouts. The Communist Party dominated a big unemployment movement, the Unemployed Councils. And young CP members who had acquired certain skills on the campuses in the organization of the movement—learning how to speak at meetings, make motions and do other things which the average person is afraid to even think of—went into the unemployment movement where they got further experience in organizational work.

When a slight upturn in industry came in the mid-thirties, they were sent into the factories. Many of these leaders of the Stalinist movement, as well as the Socialist Party to a lesser extent, became prominent. Some of their leaders in auto and other mass production industries began as former students, former Unemployed Council workers. I bet if a statistical record could be made, a large percentage of their most dynamic and influential people had had some experience on the colleges, as well as in the Unemployed Councils.

I always think of that whenever I hear this chatter of the sectarian groups who make a hue and cry about leaving the campus and getting into the factories. Theoretically it's all right in the long run, because you certainly can't make a revolution on the campuses. For one reason, they don't have the industrial power. But workers recruited and convinced of the historical trend toward socialism and committed to it—and who have also had the benefit of a college education and experience in college organizations—can become very effective leaders in the mass movement of the workers.

And the same holds true for the unemployment movement, which will become, in my opinion, a big phenomenon in a period of serious economic crisis in this country.

I think we should think of our work on the campuses as preparatory work for the coming upsurge of the workers movement, in which the people who were recruited and trained as socialists can play a great role. Both their education and their experience in organization will be very important factors and can be extremely advantageous in a surging new movement of workers—whether in unemployed movements or in unions or both.

Organizational independence

FINKEL: How did the YPSL and the Young Communists organize? Were they independent of the Socialist Party and the Communist Party? Were they controlled from the top down?

CANNON: They were completely controlled. The theory of the Communist youth organization as laid down in Russia by the Bolsheviks was applied only on paper here. The formula was an organization of young people politically subordinate, but organizationally independent of the party. That was the formula. But in practice it didn't amount to much here. The control of the party was pretty absolute—as you see it now in the Communist Party.

The Young Communist League in my day in the twenties played no independent role. It was an appendage of the party. And the able young people in it were only too eager to get through with their YCL experience and get into the party, into the party faction fights where the real action was.

Max Shachtman, for instance, was the editor of the *Young Worker,* which was the Young Communist League paper. And Martin Abern was national secretary. As I say, they considered themselves as going through an apprenticeship. Their real interest was in the party. They belonged to the Cannon faction, as it was called, in the early twenties.

I didn't take much interest in YPSL in the twenties, so I can't speak from direct experience. But I think it was pretty much the same thing. Sort of shepherded by the party.

YPSL broke loose in the thirties. The YPSLs turned left politically faster than the Socialist Party So that when we came to the showdown in 1937—at the time we were in the Socialist Party[6]—at the national convention held in Philadelphia, the Trotskyists had a majority in YPSL, and we took a majority of YPSL with us.

I think YPSL at that time had about 1,000 members. Hal Draper was the national secretary, and he stayed with us a few years and then went out with the Shachtmanites. He remained a YPSL at heart. The last I heard of him, he was still operating on the campus.

YSA a new phenomenon

The Young Socialist Alliance of today is an entirely new phenomenon, as far as my experience can judge, by its composition, its general activity and in practically every other way.

The earlier youth movements were not nearly as serious as the party itself. A great many of them seemed really to be playing with ideas for awhile before turning their attention to some career. I used to hear the expression "career-oriented." That meant that they were not aiming to fight the rest of their lives for socialism; they were looking for a good job or profession or something of that sort.

This was true even of the left-wing young socialists that we recruited in 1937. The great majority were not serious. The Shachtman and Burnham gang took the majority of them and they were fully entitled to them because they weren't made for a serious party.

6. **Trotskyists in the Socialist Party.** The American Trotskyists joined the SP in 1936 in order to gain a hearing among the radicalizing young people in the left wing of the party. In June 1937, the leadership of the SP began wholesale expulsions of the left wing forces in the party, leading in December 1937–January 1938 to the founding of the Socialist Workers Party by those expelled from the SP.

Our youth movement of today benefits greatly from the tradition that we carried over with us from the Communist Party—the Leninist concepts of the movement. A serious movement of people who join and commit themselves to fight for socialism under any circumstances. And the conception of a professional staff.

This concept was not originated in America. It came entirely from the Bolsheviks like many of our other best ideas. I don't know how big a staff we now have in the party and the youth movement, but in the movement before the Russian revolution everything was a very casual affair. The national office consisted of a national secretary, a couple of stenographers, a bookkeeper and a lecture bureau and that was about it. The IWW national office consisted of a general secretary, Vincent St. John, in the days when I used to go there. St. John, a stenographer and a bookkeeper and that was it.

FINKEL: That was all?

How the IWW was organized

CANNON: That was the national office of the IWW. There was a tremendous movement of what was called the "decentralizers," who thought even that was too damn big of a bureaucracy to have hanging around their necks. They conducted a bitter fight to transform the national office into simply a communications center where the locals would send communications that would be forwarded to others. In 1913 we had a knock-down-drag-out fight at the convention with the decentralizers.

In addition to the national office of St. John, the stenographer and the bookkeeper, you see, there was a General Executive Board of I think seven members who met about once every three months. The rest of the time they went out as field organizers, sometimes on the payroll, sometimes not, according to how the finances stood out in the field.

And the decentralizers howled their heads off at the 1913 convention (that's the last one I attended) demanding that the organization be decentralized and that all power be in the hands of the rank and file. The rank and file meant the locals. Each local for itself. They should communicate with each other through the national office, sending letters to Chicago. And Chicago would forward a copy. On such things they argued for days and days.

Well, they were defeated by St. John, who had an overwhelming personality. He was an organizer of the first quality and knew that organization required some centralization. And then St. John was succeeded by Bill Haywood[7]—in 1914 I think.

Haywood went to prison in 1918, and the decentralizers took over by a quiet operation in 1919. They adopted a motion that the national officers, the national secretary and the national organizer (who was not in the office but out in the field all the time) and any other national officials should serve only one term. Just about the time they got their hands into their jobs, they'd be out and the new force would come in. And that was one, but not the main reason I think, for the decline of the IWW after the big persecution[8] during the First World War and the prison terms of the top leaders and so on.

I think there's some kind of myth or legend about the IWW which is entertained maybe by a lot of students. They've heard so much about it. And there was a wonderful militancy in the IWW.

But the IWW after the big persecution where hundreds were jailed, after 1920 or 1921, had no action whatever in the industrial field that anybody can recall. When the time came for the IWW project of industrial unions to be realized, it came from below in the mass production industries and the IWW was standing on the sidelines with their mouths open.[9] They had nothing to do with it except as participants under different auspices.

7. **Bill Haywood.** William (Big Bill) Haywood was the IWW's leading agitator and spokesman. Haywood became an avid defender of the Bolshevik revolution and died in the Soviet Union in 1928 after living there throughout most of the decade. Jim Cannon roomed with Bill Haywood when both were delegates to international meetings in Moscow.

8. **The "big persecution."** During the period of U.S. participation in World War I, especially after the Bolshevik revolution, members of the IWW and other pro-labor and antiwar activists were arrested in large numbers and held in jail. After the war, the hysteria steadily increased under Democratic Party Attorney General A. Mitchell Palmer, leading in January 1920 to a series of nationally-coordinated mass arrests and deportations of radicals.

9. **Industrial unions in the mass production industries.** The unionization of the mass of industrial workers into powerful organizations such as the United Steel Workers and the United Auto Workers was accomplished in the thirties and early forties by the Congress of Industrial Organizations (CIO).

FINKEL: One of the questions we often get is how students can be effective. They don't see the working class in motion and they often wonder what difference it makes or matters if they join the YSA. It's very abstract to them. How would you answer a question like that?

CANNON: Well, I would say a good beginning is to adopt a historical view of society. Try to get a clear idea of where we came from and where from all indications we're heading.

And the second would be, as a beginning, to read my pamphlet *America's Road to Socialism* and get the beginning of a concept of the historical collision that's in the making and that's not so far away. Students today are going to face such crises that they will see that any plan they've made for a settled, secure and a quiet career of making a lot of money is not in the cards anymore.

Things are going to blow up. There's either going to be a revolution that transforms the whole social system or there isn't going to be anything left.

And we don't need to say that with any exaggeration or hysteria at all. That's what practically all scholars and other observers of society take for granted. One of the most common expressions you read in historical prognoses these days is "In the future, if there is to be a future of the human race, it has to be different."

If you think, on top of everything else, that they've already got enough atomic weapons of various kinds that can reach all points on the globe at the push of a button—enough to destroy the whole human race seven or eight times over. And if you think that every time there's any sign of a sharp international crisis everybody gets apprehensive about who's going to drop the first atom bomb and what will follow it, then you realize that the old slogan of the days before the First World War—that is, the historical perspective is either socialism or barbarism—is even more true today.

Today everybody with any knowledge of things will have to admit that the perspective is either socialism or annihilation. That's even worse than barbarism, because theoretically you can recover from a new barbarism. But nobody's yet recovered from the ashes of atomic destruction.

I believe that young people are particularly responsive to discussions of that kind. And that's not some pipe dream at all. These are the demonstrable facts of life in the year 1974. The only worthwhile thing for a young person to commit herself or himself to is a movement to make possible the continuation of the human race and its further evolution, development and progress. That can be stated seriously as a practical proposition. "That's the way it is," as Walter Cronkite says when he winds up his evening news.

We couldn't say that with such assurance in the old days. One of the hardest things to answer was, "Well it's a good idea, but we'll never realize it. People will never agree to it." or "It's a hundred years away, so what's the use of worrying about it?"

But that's not the case today. The young generation you're talking to is going to see it one way or another. And you may be able to decide. That's really a terrific thought—that one single person may make the difference.

I heard on TV several years ago an interview with the philosopher Bertrand Russell who was greatly disturbed about the development of atomic weapons and was agitated about the danger of them. He had accumulated considerable knowledge of atomic weapons' potential for destruction.

He was asked, "What do you consider is your main concern?" He hesitated a moment, and he said, "I want to see the human race continue." And then he was asked, "And what do you think are the odds?" He replied, "About four to six as I see it right now"—about four to six, for the chances of the human race continuing. The next question was, "What can we do about it?" And he said, "The only thing I know is to keep working and struggling to change the odds."

I always thought of this as a very perceptive statement of the dilemma facing the young generation today. Not at all what it was 50 or 100 years ago. In some of my last speeches before I fell into retirement, so to speak, I quoted this along with opinions of other informed people. I found a great response to that formulation and developed it further.

I said, "Suppose by our efforts we can push the odds up to 50-50, which is easily conceivable. By our efforts we can make it five to five instead of four to six! There's a point where one feather on one side of the scale or the other can make a difference on the basic question. It doesn't matter who we are, or where we're situated, or what we do; any one of us can make that difference."

It's a sobering formulation, isn't it? And yet, I personally feel that it is not at all a fantastic formulation. I feel that the human race is at the point where it's got to decide and hasn't too much time to do it. I'm almost certain it's going to be decided one way or another in the lifetime of the new generation entering the world of political action.

And then you should consider that the human race hasn't yet had a real chance to show what it's capable of doing. It has been the victim throughout the millenia of the social system that it has been born into. Humanity has done pretty well in coping with the problems of nature, of science and technology, but we have not yet gained control of our own social system. Nobody knows what's possible. But we can say *all* things are possible if we had an organized, consciously directed and planned organization of society and production.

It just staggers the mind to think of what could be done if everybody in the world had access to all the knowledge that has been accumulated over the ages and had an opportunity to develop the latent talents that everybody has to a greater or lesser extent. How much waste in the social system could be eliminated and converted to constructive uses! Good God! Just think, in this country we throw away $80 billion a year on weapons of destruction. Just that alone, to say nothing of what we throw away on useless advertising, dirty tricks and things of that sort in politics. God almighty!

And then, as Trotsky said in one of his articles in *Literature and Revolution*, humanity under socialism for the first time will begin to understand itself and to consciously develop to its best capacity. That's never been done. That requires a change in the social system. And he predicted that we will develop the human race to the point where the average person reaches the height of an Aristotle, or a Goethe or a Marx, and beyond that, new peaks will rise.

Well, I think a young person listening to those arguments will have a hard time coming up with an answer to them. You've got to pose the question flatly: that there's a danger that the human race may not continue; and if it's going to continue it's got to take control of its own social system and reorganize it and plan and eliminate the constant day-to-day danger of annihilation.

FINKEL: Then they ask you how do you do it?

CANNON: Well, we're not going to say it's an easy thing to do. It's a lifetime job for each and everyone of us. But the thing that inspires one's life and makes it worth living in the face of all this calamitous danger everywhere, uncertainties and insecurity, is to commit yourself to an effort to change it. And not to belittle oneself and think you don't count. You may be the decisive factor.

FINKEL: Thank you very much, Jim.

CANNON: Thank you for giving me a chance to sound off. I don't get on the soapbox much any more these days. If I can convey any suggestion to you it's this—the longer you live in this fight, the more determined you are to try to win it and the more confident you are that the human race will survive.

THOUGHTS ON SOCIALISM AND BLACK LIBERATION

The following are excerpts from a discussion between James P. Cannon and Maceo Dixon and Omari Musa. Dixon is the cochairman of the 1974 Socialist Workers Party National Campaign Committee. Musa is the Socialist Workers Party candidate for Congress in California's 28th C.D. The discussion took place July 7, 1974.

CANNON: I'm more convinced than ever that there is no solution to the social problems in this country and Western Europe short of a thoroughgoing revolution. And that will require cooperation of all the varied elements who are oppressed by this society.

That doesn't stop us from supporting movements of a special kind, like the women's liberation movement, the Black movement for self-determination, the Puerto Rican movement, and all sections who are especially oppressed. But these struggles should be pushed toward the goal of cooperation for the elimination of the capitalist system.

This is certainly more urgent now than ever, when the capitalist rulers have the means of actually destroying the human race.

That's no longer considered a fantasy. You read frequently about scholars and even politicians talking about the future, and they use the expression, "in the future—if there is to be a future." It's a way of saying they're unsure about the prospects of humanity.

The real meaning of this hasn't yet been fully appreciated by our movement. I recall reading, at the time when they were just discovering the secret of the hydrogen bomb, that Albert Einstein wrote a letter to the president in which he said it is now theoretically possible to destroy all life on earth. I don't think we have yet fully assimilated the significance of that statement.

This possible annihilation is no longer a matter of theory, it's a matter of more or less common knowledge. So much so that a popular movie, *On the Beach*, was made in which an unexplained atomic explosion took place in one part of the world, and it couldn't be ascertained where it came from. Each power that held nuclear weapons suspected the other and began firing back. First thing you knew, the bombs, the fallout, and all the rest wiped everything out.

I think the only thing that deters a man like Nixon from actually pushing the button even in a fit of pique is that he himself would be one of the victims. Imagine a man with such cynical lack of any human consideration as shown repeatedly in the Watergate exposures.

I recall that our movement talked about the danger of the Third World War for a long time without realizing what we were doing, because we were really talking about a global war in conventional terms. But you can't have another full-scale war like that.

What we need in this country is a generation that is aroused by the socialist idea somewhat as they were in the times of Eugene V. Debs. Where people think of socialism as practical and as an immediate necessity.

Debs got about a million votes in 1912, which would be equal to about three million votes today—or actually more because that was before women's suffrage. If we had a couple of million people in this country committed to socialism today they wouldn't be committed to an idea for the distant future, they would be committed for tomorrow, for a showdown struggle with the ruling class.

Black Trotskyists

I would like to see the development of a large cadre of Black Trotskyists—many more than we have already.

Real socialists, not people who have only one particular angle of the Black movement that interests them, but people who are committed to the idea that we have to make a socialist revolution in this country and we haven't got all the time in the world to do it. We've got to do it in our lifetimes. Certainly in the lifetime of the new generation entering the field.

That conviction will also inspire a hundred times more energy and confidence than if we think, well, if we don't do it the next generation will take care of it.

We should be able to convince ten thousand people—a couple of thousand at least of Black people—that socialism is the foremost issue of our times and is on the agenda. The alternative is a strong probability of annihilation of life on earth.

Once you have a cadre that size, its growth would be phenomenal, because its activity would not be casual, like a fraternal order of some kind. They'd be people fighting for their lives and the lives of humanity in a socialist world.

DIXON: What do you think about the recent exposures printed in *The Militant* showing how the FBI infiltrates the Black movement in order to attempt to crush it?

CANNON: I think that what *The Militant* has done, and the suit against the government that the SWP is waging, demonstrate the correctness of utilizing all democratic processes that are available.

This approach is contrary to the traditions of the radical movement of the generation that I grew up in. The IWW (Industrial Workers of the World) and others at that time had the attitude that the whole damn thing is a fake—there's no democracy and there's no sense in trying to get anything from the ruling class through those channels. That the only way you can get anything is by direct action, strikes, and revolution.

But the fact is that we live under a bourgeois democracy. It's pretty badly tarnished lately by the Watergate news, but we're correctly using the courts to force them to make more of these revelations, which *The Militant* is publicizing.

I think it's very good propaganda and should evoke wide interest in the Black community. We can show them, look what the government's been doing against the Black movement, and the SWP has brought a suit against them and is forcing them to reveal more.

Black party

DIXON: The Socialist Workers Party raises the slogan for a Black party based on the Black community. Why do you think this is important?

CANNON: It's in the same category as our call for a labor party. It's a first step toward the idea of independent political action.

What kind of response does it get?

DIXON: I get a very good response when I raise it in speaking around the country. People agree with the idea of endorsing Black candidates. Most say that it's not possible to build a Black party now but they hope to build it in the future. This is especially the line taken by Black Democrats.

CANNON: Yes, they say they couldn't get elected to office right now through a Black party.

You know, the old populist movement was basically a combination of poor farmers and workers. It was very strong in the Midwest. They decided to be "practical" just for one time. In 1896 they decided to support the Democratic candidate and not run their own campaign. They got a number of their leaders elected to office as Democrats. This was their ruin. They finally faded from the scene.

'Playing it smart'

There used to be quite a vigorous movement of discontented farmers and workers in the upper Midwest—Minnesota, the Dakotas, Nebraska, Kansas. They were mainly farmers.

They aroused considerable strength and were becoming a power, until a fellow named A. C. Townley came along with the idea of playing it smart. His idea was to transform their movement into the Nonpartisan League, an organization that would support one or another candidate of the Democrats or Republicans, depending on which appeared to offer the most concessions.

They elected quite a number of congressmen and even some governors.

The Socialist Party was very strong in that whole territory and they went along with the Nonpartisan League. The net result was the wiping out of the independent movement altogether. A few individuals got offices out of it and that was it.

In 1934 Upton Sinclair, who had been a lifetime socialist, suddenly got the bright idea he could jump over the difficulties of independent political action and run for governor on the Democratic ticket.

He called for a new movement named the EPIC movement, which stood for "End Poverty in California." They used to say all kinds of things of an extremely radical nature.

He got a great majority of the Socialist Party members behind him and won the Democratic Party nomination. He came within an inch of winning. The general opinion was that he was robbed of the election.

His chief "accomplishment" was to virtually dissolve the Socialist Party of California. It never got together again. When I went out to California in 1936 the Socialist Party was just a hollow shell. It had once been quite a force.

The EPIC movement survived for a few years and in 1938 its candidate, Culbert Olson, was elected governor on the Democratic ticket. In 1942 I think the Republicans took over. The EPIC movement didn't leave a trace; it's not even remembered today.

These movements that try to cut corners on the basic principle of *independent* political action always end up paying heavily for it.

Where the power is

I sometimes wonder whether our movement today, which is predominantly young, fully realizes where the power lies in this country. The power is in the working class. When we talk about the Black population, we're talking about workers, mainly.

Workers are not always the first to move in a radicalization. When the crisis struck in 1928–29 there was quite a surge of radicalization at first in intellectual and literary circles. There wasn't a move on the part of the workers. They were atomized, they were unorganized, had no unions in auto or steel or electrical manufacture.

A few desperate strikes here and there were crushed.

It gave rise to a feeling that the workers would never move.

In 1934 they finally got enough of hardship, wage cuts one after another, mass unemployment. There were three big strikes in a row at the same time—the San Francisco general strike, the Minneapolis Teamsters strike, and the Toledo Auto-Lite strike. All very militant and successful, involving people who had never been organized before.

In 10 years this American working class, which was supposed to be unable to do anything, had organized auto almost from top to bottom. There was the sit-down strike in Flint in 1936–37. The strike against "Little Steel" in the same year, when the police fired on the workers and killed a dozen or more of them. Big Steel had signed a contract with the CIO without even a strike. Within 10 years basic industry in this country was organized.

I've often thought what would have been possible in this country if we had had a revolutionary party then, if the Communist Party had been a revolutionary party. It grew greatly in membership. It got as high as 80,000 members, I think.

But that upsurge coincided with Moscow's turn toward peaceful coexistence, the CP's support for Roosevelt, and all the rest. The Communist Party, instead of being an inspirer and leader of these young militants who were ready for anything, put a damper on the struggle.

Anything was possible

I think anything was possible in the late 1930s. By God, workers who'd never opened their mouths in Flint suddenly decided to go on strike, shut down the goddamn place, and occupied it. They occupied the GM plants in Flint and organized a women's battalion to parade around town raising hell until General Motors capitulated. The same thing happened in Chrysler and eventually in Ford.

Ford was supposed to have a permanent fiefdom. He had a paternalistic regime. Back in the 1920s he gave $5-a-day minimum wage to workers coming off the farms and out of the bayous. There was one catch to it. They had to be under strict supervision of Mr. Ford. He had community organizations supervising their conduct, what organizations they belonged to, whether they went to church, etc. The workers were so pleased with the $5 a day that they went along with that. No unionism.

Another big reform of Ford's was to give some ex-convicts a chance at $5 a day. The catch here was that these convicts happened to be goons and their task was to look out for anybody opening his mouth about unionism.

They didn't argue with him, they beat the hell out of him and threw him out. That kept Ford out of the union drive until he was the last one left. In 1941 they finally shut down Ford's River Rouge plant and unionized this holdout.

The point is the power the workers have once they rise up and go into action. Then it's no longer a debate, it's a fight. There's no question of where the potential and ultimate power is. The only way that the workers can be headed off in a revolutionary situation is to be deceived or misled.

I think we have to convince a few thousand Black workers that socialism and revolution and liberation are all the same thing and that it's on the agenda, and that it's possible and *necessary* for survival to have a socialist society in their lifetime before it's too late.

When you get a few thousand Black workers inspired with that idea and that conviction, you're on the road. And when there's a corresponding development among the white workers, with ten or twenty thousand white worker members of our party, you've got the nucleus of an invincible force right there.

QUESTIONS OF AMERICAN RADICAL HISTORY

The following interview was conducted at James P. Cannon's home in Los Angeles July 16.

Sidney Lens is a labor historian who was active in the anti-Vietnam war movement. He is also an editor of Liberation magazine.

LENS: I interviewed Earl Browder[1] before he died. What was your reaction to him personally?

CANNON: Well, that's quite a story, because I knew him for many years.

LENS: Yes, I know, but did you like him personally?

CANNON: For a long time we worked together.

LENS: He never joined the Wobblies (Industrial Workers of the World—IWW), did he?

CANNON: I don't think so. He became a disciple of Foster.[2] Foster came through Kansas City, I think it was in 1913. He had been a Wobbly who had gone to France and had become converted to syndicalism. He came back and made a tour of the IWW locals, trying to convince them of his ideas of 'boring from within' the AFL (American Federation of Labor). Browder was one of his converts from Kansas City.

LENS: Did he try to convert you?

CANNON: No.

LENS: Why not?

CANNON: I didn't run into him personally. I don't know whether Browder had been a Wobbly or not. I had been traveling around the country shortly before that and had been out of Kansas City. I knew he was a radical.

LENS: What made Browder become a Stalinist?

CANNON: That's a long story. What made all the others become Stalinists?

LENS: Was it a matter of just belonging to something big?

CANNON: Yes.

LENS: He told me that he disliked Trotsky personally. He was quite senile when I saw him, and he spoke very cryptically. He gave the impression that the biggest basis for not joining with Trotsky was that he considered Trotsky a show-off and very egotistical.

CANNON: When the first world war broke out for this country in 1917, Browder had been working in the (food and farm) cooperative movement. He was an accountant by profession. I think he was impressed by the cooperative movement, which at that time there was quite a sentiment for.

He had been to New York. He may have been influenced by Emma Goldman and Alexander Berkman's demonstrations of opposition to the war. He came back to Kansas City. He and his two brothers and his brother-in-law, Bob Sullivan, made an open demonstration against the entry into the war with leaflets. They were promptly arrested. He got a year in the Missouri State Penitentiary. They got out about 1918.

Recruited Browder

By that time I had become a communist. I saw them immediately after they came out. They had

1. Earl Browder was general secretary of the American Communist Party from 1930 to 1945.

2. William Z. Foster was the most important trade-union figure to join the early Communist Party.

no inclination toward the communist movement because it was harebrained. There was some truth in that. There was a large element of harebrains in the new communist movement. But I think it's safe to say that I convinced him there was fundamental merit in it. And he became a communist.

In the fall of 1918 we decided to start a paper in Kansas City. It had no political allegiance at its start, but it was an exponent of the Russian revolution and defense of class-war prisoners and so on. Browder was the first editor and I worked very closely with him, promoting the idea of the paper and then getting started on it.

Along about early summer of 1919 he and his brothers had to go back to serve a federal sentence in Leavenworth, Kans., and I had to take over the paper as editor.

We remained close associates while he was in prison. I became rather prominent in the new communist movement. I was elected to the central committee at the first Bridgeman, Mich., convention in the spring of 1920 and became organizer of the St. Louis–Southern Illinois coal district for the party. A few months after that I was moved to Cleveland to become editor of a paper called the *Toiler*, which was a continuation of the *Ohio Socialist*.

(Alfred) Wagenknecht and his group had control of the state (Socialist Party) organization and they took the paper along with them when the split came (the split of the left wing from the SP). A few months later they decided to move the paper to New York and change the name to the *Worker* and I went along with that. That would be in the late fall of 1920. Eventually it became the *Daily Worker*. So if you want to have a record of my sins, you can say I was the original editor of the *Daily Worker*.

December 1938.

LENS: Yes, I know that record.

CANNON: Browder was in prison till the spring of 1921. He wasn't known to the leadership of the party. It was on my recommendation that he was brought to New York. He became right away the assistant of Foster, who had also at that time decided to join the party clandestinely.

They decided to start a monthly magazine, the *Labor Monthly*, in Chicago, with Foster as editor and Browder as managing editor. We were close together all that time up until Foster and I had a falling out—in 1925, I think it was.

LENS: What was that all about?

CANNON: I tell the story in my book *The First Ten Years of American Communism* in reply to some of (Theodore) Draper's questions. The split took place rather dramatically at a plenary meeting, right down the middle of the Foster-Cannon group. People like Bill Dunne, Arne Swabeck, and others came with me. Browder and (Jack) Johnstone and others went with Foster in this split, which was never fully healed, although we had relations later. That amounted to a personal falling out in 1925. That would be about 12 years after I first met him.

LENS: Would you consider Browder a creative person in that period, independent?

CANNON: No.

LENS: Did he always have to attach himself to somebody, like to Foster or you?

CANNON: He wasn't by nature a leader or a politician. There was never such a thing as a Browder group in the party. There was a Foster group, and a Cannon group, and a Ruthenberg group. But he was a very energetic and intelligent, capable worker.

LENS: Was there anything in the twenties similar to the present counter-culture amongst the youth?

CANNON: Not to my knowledge.

LENS: What were the main reasons for the failure of the Communist Party (CP) to take off? I know that's a big story, but do you think they were mainly subjective reasons?

CANNON: Well, of course, first there were the persecutions, quite severe in the first few years. The party was driven underground. Next there was a sharp economic depression and then an ascending boom that continued throughout the twenties. That wasn't a very fertile field for communism to expand. And it was a new movement with a lot to learn.

LENS: Did you anticipate the depression of 1929?

CANNON: Well, we kept forecasting it.

LENS: Yes, you kept forecasting it from about 1922 on.

CANNON: So we were eventually vindicated in 1929.

LENS: But did you anticipate that particular depression and that it would come through the stock market crash?

CANNON: I wouldn't say specifically so, but the Lovestoneites[3] wrote a document on American exceptionalism. The Comintern (Communist International) was just beginning its left turn. They wrote a document on American exceptionalism. That's what they called it. Sort of exempting America from the world trend for the time being.

And we wrote a counter-document in collaboration with the Fosterites that we presented at the Sixth Congress of the Comintern in 1928. It was called "The Right Danger in the American Party." There you'll see that we took a rather radical approach to the whole question, including the economy.

LENS: When the depression came, what were your personal reactions? Did you feel that America was moving close to an actual revolution?

CANNON: I can't say that I did.

LENS: Then what was your reaction?

CANNON: Like most everybody else, stunned.

LENS: Stunned?

Workers atomized

CANNON: Yes, it was so severe. It was hard to see an immediate revolution. The workers were atomized. The organized labor movement had lost ground in the twenties. The unions had fewer than three million members at the time of the crash and they began losing more after that.

LENS: Did the CP really believe that a revolution impended?

CANNON: At that time they were in the midst of the "third period."[4] So they were running hog-wild for a while, but they weren't getting much response to that appeal.

LENS: Was your organization called the Communist League of America at first, or was it called Communist Party Majority or Left Opposition?

CANNON: Communist League of America (Opposition). The Lovestoneites called themselves Communist Party (Majority Group).[5]

LENS: Then you dropped the word "opposition" eventually.

CANNON: Eventually, yes. But for four years we continued to direct our agitation mainly to the Communist Party.

LENS: Were you disappointed in the results?

CANNON: Well, we were trying to recruit our primary cadre and we recruited more than a hundred people to begin with. I guess we had a couple

3. Jay Lovestone was secretary of the CP in the 1920s. He headed a rightist faction in the party that was aligned internationally with Bukharin. In 1928, Lovestone carried out the expulsion of the American Trotskyists from the CP. When Stalin turned on his rightist allies in 1929, Lovestone was demoted from his post and expelled.

The Lovestone group maintained itself until the outbreak of World War II and then dissolved. Lovestone subsequently became an anticommunist expert for the AFL-CIO bureaucracy.

4. The "third period" was a schema proclaimed by the Stalinists in 1928 according to which capitalism was in its final period of collapse. Following from this schema, the Comintern's tactics during the next six years were marked by ultra-leftism, adventurism, sectarian "red" unions, and opposition to forming united fronts with other working-class organizations.

5. The Communist League of America (Opposition) was the organization formed by Cannon and others who were expelled from the Communist Party in 1928 for supporting the program of the Left Opposition in the Soviet CP, led by Leon Trotsky.

of hundred or a little more by 1934 and then we got into the Minneapolis strike and that gave us a big boost. It identified us as workers in the mass movement.

Then came the fusion with the Musteites[6] in the same year. So it was sort of a period of expansion in the later thirties.

LENS: What happened then in the relatively large mass movement before World War II and during World War II? Did you feel that there was something impeding your development or your progress, or were you going too slow, or what?

CANNON: Do you mean our organization?

LENS: Yes.

CANNON: Our big obstacle was the Communist Party. It had complete domination of what there was of the radical movement. The SP was an empty shell. And we were isolated. The membership of the Communist Party largely identified Stalin with the Comintern. And whatever the Comintern said was the law. But we kept recruiting one here and one there until we'd built up quite a cadre of capable people.

LENS: Why didn't you take over the Communist Party? Why didn't the majority come over to your point of view? Must a radical party have the support of a government in some foreign country to survive or prosper?

CANNON: The Comintern represented the Russian revolution in the minds of the American communists. The Comintern said we were counterrevolutionaries and that Trotsky was a fascist, a traitor, and everything else; and they accepted that.

LENS: From a theoretical point of view, though, Marxism is supposed to be the science of revolution, and your estimate of events was more lucid than Browder's, say and yet here were ten or twenty thousand communists to whom you couldn't get through. Their emotions were much stronger than their intellectual probing.

CANNON: That's true; it took a long time for us to break through.

LENS: Is that a handicap that the left can always expect, that emotion plays a bigger role than science of revolution?

CANNON: The pull of a radical organization that is dominant in the field is almost gravitational. The average worker and activist doesn't want to be connected with some little sect on the sidelines. He wants to be where the action is.

Muste group

LENS: Did the Muste group make any sensational spurt in its early days, or was it growing about like your group?

CANNON: It was growing about like ours. Muste was a remarkable personal character. He was a preacher, you know, to start with.

In 1917, as a minister in Boston, he went to Lawrence, Mass., and got into the textile strike there and became the head of it. Next, if I'm correct, he became the head of the textile workers union, or what was left of it.

Then he started the Brookwood Labor College in New York State, which quite a number of people attended, and he recruited some of them. Out of that he developed the Conference for Progressive Labor Action and recruited people here and there. Then this organization developed an unemployed movement of its own.

The Communist Party dominated the main unemployment movement in the big cities, the Unemployed Councils. The Musteites organized around the fringes rather effectively, in Pennsylvania, Ohio, and other places. The Unemployed Leagues, they called them. Through all these operations Muste accumulated a cadre.

We were greatly impressed with their actions in the Toledo Auto-Lite strike in 1934, at the same time that we were occupied with the Teamsters' fight in Minneapolis. They had done an unprecedented thing. Their leaders there—Sam Pollock, Ted Selander, and Art Preis—were in the unemployment movement, the Unemployed League of the Musteites. And they organized to support the strike.

Contrary to the custom of the unemployed being recruited as strikebreakers, they became

6. In December 1934 the Communist League of America fused with the American Workers Party, led by A.J. Muste, to form the Workers Party of the United States.

the most militant supporters of the strike. They practically led the strike. We were tremendously impressed by that, and it led to our negotiations with them for fusion. Meanwhile Muste was turning to the left politically, so there wasn't much trouble in bringing about a unification.

Some of the people that Muste had attracted—such as (J.B.S.) Hardman and (Louis) Budenz and a few others—wouldn't go along with it, but Muste decided to do it and he brought along a majority of his people and it gave the movement quite a boost.

LENS: Did you expect a revolution in the 1930s—that capitalism would collapse?

CANNON: I can't say that I expected it, but looking back on it now, as I have said many times, anything was possible in the thirties. After the workers recovered from their paralysis. In the first four or five years they were simply stunned, they didn't know what to do. But beginning with Minneapolis in 1934, three strikes—Minneapolis, the San Francisco general strike, and the Auto-Lite strike in Toledo—seemed to give the impetus needed for a new movement. And it began to develop by leaps and bounds.

LENS: What stopped it?

Tremendous upheaval

CANNON: The American Communist Party.

The industrial union movement developed millions of members and John L. Lewis, recognizing the tide, turned toward it and gave quite effective leadership for a time. The sit-down strikes in Flint, Mich., and the organization of General Motors and Ford represented a tremendous upheaval. That was accomplished in a few years.

LENS: When you say the Communist Party stopped it, in what way?

CANNON: The Communist Party was the dominant force in the radical movement. They dominated the unemployed movement and by that time there developed a radical movement on the campuses, which they also dominated. And they trained some cadres in the unemployment and student movements who took part in various actions.

You know, the average worker is afraid to stand up and make a motion in a meeting. They aren't accustomed to that. The CP trained a whole cadre of people who could stand up and make motions and parliamentary moves, and run meetings, and things of this sort.

In the mid-thirties there was a certain upsurge out of the depression. Not a real economic recovery, but a revival. They began to open factories and take some people back to work. And the Communist Party colonized a lot of their people in the strategic industries and their radical talk appealed widely. They were competitors for control of the auto workers union for a while.

Right in the middle of this came the turn of the Comintern toward the right. The "third period" had passed and the Kremlin began turning over toward conservatism and naturally the Communist Party just carried it out here in the United States to the letter.

I believe that if the Communist Party had remained a revolutionary party, it could have made great things out of that mass movement of the thirties.

LENS: If you go back to the Russian revolution, you also had a Menshevik group, and the Bolsheviks were a minority in relation to the Mensheviks, and yet they were able to pull people away from them. Why weren't the Trotskyists able to pull people from the Stalinists here? You also had capable people, you also knew how to make motions in meetings and all the rest of that, and probably were more dedicated.

Excluded

CANNON: Unquestionably. But we didn't have the numbers. The Communist Party excluded us from every movement they controlled, like the unemployed movement. A hungry unemployed member of the Trotskyist organization couldn't get into the Unemployed Councils because the Stalinists branded him a "counterrevolutionary."

The CP formed alliances with other radicals and socialists in the League Against War and Fascism, but we were not admitted to it. So although we expanded somewhat with the success of the Minneapolis strikes, the fusion with the Musteites, and the entry into the Socialist Party,[7] which gained us quite a group of new members, we were still a small minority in comparison to the Communist Party.

LENS: You expected quite a bit more from the entry in the Socialist Party, didn't you, than you eventually got?

CANNON: We won over the majority of the Young People's Socialist League.

LENS: I know, but you really expected to become an important mass party.

CANNON: We expected the Socialist Party itself to grow and that we would grow with it.

LENS: Why didn't it?

CANNON: The competition of the Communist Party, and partly the inadequacy of its leadership, I guess.

LENS: Of the Communist or Socialist leadership?

CANNON: Of the Socialist Party leadership.

LENS: But you were playing an important role in it by then. Weren't you in the Socialist leadership?

CANNON: I came out to California during that period. We soon got a majority in the state executive committee of the Socialist Party and published a weekly paper in San Francisco. The right-wingers remaining in the Socialist Party got alarmed about that and began expelling our people. And we had nothing to do but fight it out and come to a break.

LENS: Had you expected a break?

CANNON: No, we tried to prevent it.

LENS: You had hoped to remain in the Socialist Party?

CANNON: Yes, we were not ready to bring things to a head yet. But we had no choice.

LENS: Why do you think the Comintern got rid of Browder?[8] Or, to put it a different way, why didn't he adjust to the Comintern? He had been adjusting to it all his life.

CANNON: It began with his appointment as secretary. Foster was a far more publicly prominent and able man than Browder. That was his trouble. You might say he was the logical man to succeed Lovestone when they got rid of Lovestone. But by that time Stalin didn't want any able people heading national parties.

I think Browder's defects were his merits. His lack of leadership capacity was just what they wanted from him—somebody to do what they told him to do. I don't say Foster wouldn't have done it, but Foster had ideas and initiative of his own.

LENS: Did you like Foster personally?

CANNON: At first I did. I was associated with him in the political fights. But I didn't like his character.

LENS: Why?

CANNON: Why don't you like somebody? He was terribly self-centered and dishonest, when it served his purpose, and disloyal in personal relations. All the kinds of things that I especially don't like.

LENS: Getting back to Browder. He had shifted gears with the Comintern all along, and then 1946 comes along and he refuses to shift gears. How do you account for that?

CANNON: I think he was taken by surprise. He carried the conciliationism of the Kremlin bureaucracy to an extreme that they were not prepared to go to after the war ended. They were getting ready for the outbreak of the cold war, while Browder was going ahead as before.

You remember his famous statement, when he said something like, "I'm ready to shake hands

7. In 1936 the Trotskyists joined the Socialist Party in order to win over the growing left wing to revolutionary politics.

8. Browder was deposed as secretary of the CP in 1945 and expelled from the party in 1946. Except for his first few years in office (the end of the ultraleft "third period") and the brief interlude of the Stalin-Hitler pact, his regime coincided with those years in which the CP engaged in blatant class collaboration of the people's front variety.

During the World War II alliance of the U.S. and the Soviet Union, Browder ardently supported U.S. imperialism and publicly urged that the wartime no-strike pledge be continued after the war ended.

with J. Pierpont Morgan on this—to have peace, no strikes during the war, speedup, incentive pay, and all the rest."

Out of favor

It's remarkable how easily the Stalinists disposed of him. They didn't even have to send any message directly from Moscow. All they had to do was to have somebody in France, Duclos (Jacques Duclos, longtime leader of the French Communist Party), write a piece in the French CP magazine criticizing Browder. And all the hacks in the party took that as a sign that this fellow was out of favor with the big power.

LENS: Why do you feel the Lovestoneites fell apart?

CANNON: What stages do you mean?

LENS: When they dissolved, about 1937 or 1938 (actually, 1939).

CANNON: In 1929 they took a hundred or more with them out of the Communist Party. That in itself was an indication of the tremendous power of Stalin over the party. The CP had just had a convention where the Lovestoneites had a big majority, or so they thought, because the party wasn't aware that Stalin was getting ready to dump him.

The Lovestoneites claimed to be the champions of the Comintern above all others. But the Comintern had two representatives here at the CP's 1929 convention early in the year, and the campaign against Bukharin was beginning already in Moscow. Bukharin had been their mentor and their protector, and Lovestone didn't get the signal quickly enough.

LENS: Then they survived for about 10 years. And they did have some influence in the auto workers and the ladies garment workers unions.

CANNON: As late as 1934 one of the big events in the radical movement in New York was a debate between me and Lovestone at Irving Plaza on the question of whether we should build a new international or support the Communist International. At that time he strongly supported the Comintern of Stalin. He was still, I think, hoping to convince them that he was their boy. And probably still had some idea that the Communist movement had a future here.

Some people don't have to believe things out of conviction; if they believe something is going to be a success, that's enough for them. I think that was the case with Lovestone. I think he was a careerist from the very beginning.

LENS: Let me sidetrack to another issue. The emergence of the New Left after World War II, or quite a long time after World War II, was accompanied by a tremendous counter-culture movement. Why wasn't there one in the 1930s?

CANNON: This counter-culture movement of the recent past was an intellectual student movement, wasn't it?

LENS: Yes, but you had a growing student movement in the thirties too.

CANNON: Yes, but the real power that asserted itself was a workers uprising in the 1930s. We don't have anything like that today. Nothing comparable.

LENS: In other words you feel that the students were pretty much secondary to the workers.

CANNON: In the thirties, yes.

LENS: And therefore they didn't take on characteristics of their own?

CANNON: I just don't recall them making any special mark for themselves in the thirties.

LENS: How do you account for that?

CANNON: There was a student movement, but it was mainly composed of groups affiliated to the two radical parties, the Communist Party and the Socialist Party.

I don't know whether you've heard this story, I've told it a hundred times: Among the big events on the campuses of New York in the thirties were the debates between the Draper brothers. Have you heard of that?

LENS: No. Theodore and Hal?

CANNON: Theodore Draper was an ardent Stalinist. Hal Draper was a left-wing Socialist. And they had a number of debates. I didn't attend any of them, but I heard about them.

The left wing of the Socialist Party didn't develop as a counter-cultural nut movement, but as a radical, Leninist movement. I heard Gus Tyler debate with Gil Green—who later became head of the Young Communist League—on the question of policy toward war. Green took the peaceful coexistence position of the Comintern and Tyler defended the Leninist policy. Tyler, who's now an ILGWU (International Ladies Garment Workers Union) leader, simply cut him to pieces, in my judgment.

This whole counter-culture business expressed in this New Left phenomenon seems to me like it sprang out of nowhere. And it disappeared almost as rapidly.

New Left

LENS: How do you account for the emergence of the New Left? Why didn't all those young people come into the Socialist Workers Party?

CANNON: It started with the League for Industrial Democracy, didn't it?

LENS: But that was pretty much of a dead organization.

CANNON: But they had a "Port Huron Statement" that seemed to just catch fire. It took most everybody by surprise. I certainly didn't anticipate it.

LENS: Why? Here was the SWP. Eighteen of your comrades had gone to jail for opposing World War II. You had an unsullied personal record. You had worked throughout the war rather consistently against the Stalin-Hitler pact, and then against McCarthyism. And yet, when the youth began to choose sides, they bypassed the CP and they bypassed you.

CANNON: You mustn't forget that the 1950s were a period of terrible reaction in the labor movement. In the cold war period the union bureaucrats were able with the help of the government to clean out all the Stalinists and all the other radicals from the CIO. And everything was dead on the campus. They called it the "silent generation."

We had counted greatly in the postwar period on young veterans being a natural recruiting ground for a big expansion. Instead, the soldiers came back and got the GI Bill of Rights. They went to school and they were studying to get degrees and get jobs. There was no response to radical ideas.

LENS: Did you expect a depression after the war like the depression of 1929?

CANNON: No, we were taken by surprise.

LENS: That there was no depression?

CANNON: That there was no radicalization.

LENS: But you didn't expect an economic slump in 1946–47 like Eugene Dennis did.[9]

CANNON: We expected it, but we didn't put a time limit on it. We suffered terrible reverses. We lost a lot of members in the fifties.

LENS: To what, the persecutions?

Cold war period

CANNON: The persecution, the lack of response, the inactivity of the workers. People began falling away. Our biggest struggle in the whole cold war period of the fifties was to hold our nucleus together.

LENS: How big was the SWP?

CANNON: I would say we came out of the fifties with about 500 members.

LENS: And how many members did you have in 1945?

CANNON: In 1945 we had about 3,000, I guess, because at the 1946 convention I recall we made a ceremony of initiating 1,000 new members who had been recruited since the 1944 convention. During the latter years of the war there was considerable radicalization in anticipation of the war's end and labor struggles.

But there was no sign of radicalization in the fifties, and no sign of action in the labor unions to speak of. The campuses were dead. It was the civil rights movement that sparked the rebirth of a radical movement. We oriented ourselves as much as we could to that, and we recruited some people from the campuses, and we started a youth organization again, the Young Socialist Alliance. It began

9. Eugene Dennis was general secretary of the CP in the 1950s.

to attract a cadre. In general we've been advancing ever since, not spectacularly, but rather steadily.

LENS: But my question is why did all the energy go into the organizations of the New Left? And although you've made some gains, you never made a fundamental breakthrough. How do you account for that?

CANNON: It just didn't happen.

LENS: Why? Was it something you did that was wrong?

CANNON: No, I don't know of anything we did that was wrong. In the late fifties the Khrushchev revelations opened up the Communist Party periphery. We plunged into that very determinedly. We recruited some members out of the CP itself after the Khrushchev revelations especially in Los Angeles. And since then we have confronted the Communist Party in mass movements of various kinds virtually as equals. They can't brush us aside any more.

LENS: But you never were able to become the dominant force on the left

CANNON: No.

LENS: When I asked Rennie Davis and Tom Hayden why they joined the SDS (Students for a Democratic Society) rather than the CP or the SWP, they said they felt that there was no magnetism there.

Recruited women

CANNON: We did recruit fairly substantially, and some excellent cadres. And we have recruited women comrades on a scale never before in the radical movement Forty percent of our members are women. And I think about 40 percent of our staff members are women. This takes place not as a quota policy but just naturally. So many talented women have come forward to fill this and that position.

LENS: But even with all the work you've done in the antiwar movement, you're not back to your 1945 strength yet.

CANNON: We're much stronger in the cadre sense.

LENS: Having influence.

CANNON: But I don't think we're much stronger numerically. A large number of the people we recruited during that period at the end of the war were Blacks as well as industrial workers. There was a big turnover as soon as the climate in the country turned conservative with the cold war. Then they dropped out because they expected more immediate advantages than we could offer. But this membership we have today is a pretty solid membership both in the YSA and in the SWP.

LENS: Do you anticipate a revolution in America in the near future?

CANNON: It depends on what you mean by near.

LENS: Next 10 or 15 years.

Anything possible

CANNON: I say anything is possible in this century in the years that are left of it. That's 26 years.

LENS: But you don't sound very optimistic.

CANNON: I don't want to make any categorical statements, but I say we're living in a time when capitalism is plunging toward its climactic end.

LENS: Didn't you say that in the thirties?

CANNON: I did, yes.

LENS: And in the forties?

CANNON: And in the forties.

LENS: I mean, that must sound like something peculiar when you say it every decade.

CANNON: But when you stop to think, the history of humanity is a very long one, isn't it? And a quarter of a century is only an instant in the history of the human race.

LENS: What do you see in the near future for the capitalist system?

CANNON: I see one crisis piling upon another. I don't think the capitalists have ever been in such a jam in this country as they are right now, both poltically and economically.

LENS: Yet the average man is living well compared to 40 years ago.

CANNON: Materially, you mean?

LENS: Yes.

CANNON: Yes, but they got used to the new standard and now they see the beginning of the decline and they don't like that.

One phenomenon that interests me greatly is the extraordinary development of union action among public workers. It's an entirely new phenomenon. And very widespread, very militant, and continuing.

LENS: You have two separate groups outside the CP and SWP that are radical, the New American Movement and the People's Party, which believe in the idea of a mass party. And then you have the Maoist parties, like the Revolutionary Union and the October League. Can you see the Trotskyists uniting with either of those forces?

CANNON: No.

LENS: You don't think that either one of them has a future?

CANNON: They have a future. I think this New American Movement or something like it can easily develop and have a temporary existence. But I don't think we can ever be isolated again. We will be in the midst of any kind of public mass movement that begins, and we will recruit out of it.

Left to right: Farrell Dobbs, Tom Kerry, Jim Cannon, and Louise Simpson at 1945 election rally in New York. Dobbs was SWP candidate for mayor and Simpson was SWP candidate for city council.

DISCUSSION WITH A YOUNG MEXICAN REVOLUTIONIST

The following is the transcript of an interview given by James P. Cannon to Emiliano, a member of the political bureau of the Mexican Liga Socialista (Socialist League), a sympathizing organization of the Fourth International. The interview was for *El Socialista*, the newspaper of the Socialist League.

This transcript is based on the English translation of the questions by Miguel Pendas of *The Militant's* Southwest Bureau.

The interview took place Aug. 15, less than a week before Cannon's death Aug. 21 at the age of 84.

EL SOCIALISTA: As you know, the Socialist League is a very young organization and none of its cadres has extensive experience in the labor and revolutionary movements. This lack of experience creates many political and organizational problems. One of the most important we have been grappling with is that of political education and development. We have been trying to think through what is the best way of conducting the process of systematic political education.

One of the thorny questions is whether the main emphasis should be placed on the Marxist classics, or whether we should focus more on contemporary Mexican and international problems. Do you have any suggestions on this?

CANNON: I would say both. The Socialist Workers Party has educational programs adapted to each level of development. We have classes on the history of our party, classes on the history of the Russian revolution, classes on Marxist economics. You don't have to start with *Capital;* you can take Marx's pamphlet *Value, Price, and Profit* and make a very profitable extended course out of it.

Lenin's pamphlet *Left-wing Communism, An Infantile Disorder* would make a very good subject for a class—not for just one evening, but as an extended class.

Just start somewhere. Once you get started on Marxism, you keep going. You get addicted.

EL SOCIALISTA: The problem is where to start.

CANNON: Well, Marxist economics, with *Value, Price, and Profit* is a very good start. And if you begin with Lenin's two pamphlets *Left-wing Communism, An Infantile Disorder* and *State and Revolution*, you begin to get the essence of Lenin's thoughts on wide areas.

And they're very good for beginners, especially those who are inclined toward adventuristic leaps. I think there is a tendency in Mexico toward adventurism. Young people want a revolution right away.

EL SOCIALISTA: You're absolutely right. There's a tremendous tendency toward adventurism in Mexico. It's one of the biggest problems we face.

We have been devoting a great deal of our relatively limited resources to establishing our monthly newspaper, *El Socialista*. In trying to establish an effective national publication, we are in a way going against the stream of the radical tradition in Mexico. Most of the Mexican radical groups believe that it's more important to establish local papers that have more of an influence on particular struggles.

How do you view this question of the national publication and the role it can play?

CANNON: The national view takes priority. Our paper should appeal to the whole of the Mexican working class and peasantry. That's easier said than done.

Like *The Militant*. We never think of *The Militant*

Vincent Hallinan, noted civil-liberties lawyer, and James P. Cannon at March 1, 1958, banquet in Los Angeles. Both spoke on "United Socialist Political Action in 1958 and the Outlook for American Socialists."

as a New York paper. From the very beginning, in 1928, we considered it a national and international paper. Our paper is in fact the chief educator of the movement. It's not limited to little local developments. You will never educate a national movement that way.

After you have built a big movement with a national organ, then you can have local editions, dealing with local issues.

That's my opinion. Your paper should definitely be a national paper, dealing with the affairs of government, what the government's doing, what's going on in other parts of the country, and what's going on in the world. For example, the story of the uprisings in Portugal and Greece would be good stories for Mexico, wouldn't they?

I don't think that's a progressive tendency—the idea of a movement that hasn't established a national base for itself beginning with local issues. That's putting the cart before the horse, isn't it? If you have a cadre educated in national and international affairs, then it's very easy for them to orient to local actions.

EL SOCIALISTA: The rationalization used by these people is that they'll have more influence locally if they bring out a local paper.

CANNON: But the purpose is to educate the people, and if you concentrate on local affairs, that doesn't broaden the knowledge and interests of the people. It doesn't help them see that the local affairs are only a part of what's going on in the whole world, which affects every local area.

For example, local labor strikes and uprisings are most likely prompted by national inflation right now, aren't they? So if you begin by explaining that the local workers are the victims of the national crimes of the bourgeoisie, the bankers and money sharks, it doesn't diminish your local activity, but broadens the interests of those in struggle and deepens the struggle.

EL SOCIALISTA: Is it in this sense that Lenin wrote of the newspaper as being the organizer of the revolutionary party?

CANNON: Yes, that's what it should be. It must teach about more than local incidents; it must teach the whole program of Marxism. Not all in one issue, but in installments and parts. Inflation—that's someplace to begin, right now.

The language problem

You seem to understand more English than I know of Spanish.

EL SOCIALISTA: I can read English but I can't understand much when people speak English.

CANNON: That's a weakness of our party as well as yours, languages. More people in our movement should know more than one language.

This was one thing that impressed me so strongly about the leaders of the Russian revolution when I was there in the early years. They had been exiles all over Europe and they all spoke many languages. Lenin, Trotsky, Radek, Bukharin, Zinoviev—they spoke French, German, Russian, and some even spoke English a little. Trotsky spoke a little English.

EL SOCIALISTA: This is even a factor internally in Mexico, because it accounts for unequal development in the leadership. The ones who understand English are able to develop more because they have more access to literature and conversation with comrades in other languages.

A key problem for all the sections of the Fourth International, and a particularly urgent one for us, is the development of a qualified, authoritative central leadership team. In Mexico, unfortunately, there has not been a strong tradition in this area. So in trying to develop such a leadership team we are in a sense breaking new ground.

I know you have dealt with this question extensively in your writings and attach great importance to it. Are there any comments you could make about this problem that might serve as a guide for us in our efforts?

CANNON: It's easier said than done. But reading literature on the question is the best way, and then discussing it. You should make every effort to have some of the basic works of the Trotskyist movement translated and made the subject of study classes. Even before that, if you have comrades who have read the material in another language, they could give classes in it and make a beginning that way.

What proportion of our members are students?

EL SOCIALISTA: The overwhelming majority. Probably 90 percent are high school or college students.

CANNON: Do they study languages in college?

EL SOCIALISTA: They study, but usually they don't really learn them.

CANNON: Revolutionists should take advantage of the opportunity while they're in school. Concentrate at least on one language and learn it. It would be a tremendous advantage.

EL SOCIALISTA: What role does political authority—that is, in the sense of moral authority—of the comrades play in developing a leadership team? In your writings you stress the necessity for the leadership of the party to have not only capacity, but also to have a certain moral authority. Why is this moral authority necessary?

CANNON: Authority can't be conferred; it has to be acquired. When one works a certain length of time for the party and does good work, he acquires a certain influence, which we call moral authority. It can't be organized like a game of checkers. You're dealing with people who are all different.

The main thing in my opinion is to create an atmosphere in the party where everybody is valued and everybody has a full opportunity to show what they can do for the party. And in the course of that development, certain people stand out and become leaders.

Collective leadership

And it's very fortunate if it isn't just one person who becomes a one-man leader but a group of people who combine their talents as well as their faults and make a collective leadership. That's what we need everywhere.

EL SOCIALISTA: Your writings have emphasized the importance of developing an international program and being part of a world party. We are trying to fully absorb that tradition.

We think it is of particular importance for us to establish close working relations with the comrades of the Fourth International in Latin America and also with the North American Trotskyist movement. We feel the role of the U.S. imperialists in Mexico dictates the need for such political collaboration.

Also, we feel we have already learned a great deal from the traditions and teachings of the North American movement and can learn even more. How do you see this question of collaboration between the two movements?

CANNON: First accept the general idea as you said. Well stated, in my opinion. Then we should try to find practical means of operating. I think it is very important that we have close collaboration all over the continent. One way is through direct visits.

Another way is for a wider circle of comrades to pick up the other language and read the literature and periodicals of the other countries. That would be an excellent way of keeping informed. Then those comrades can convey what they learn to the rest of the party in their own country.

Fraternal relationship

Traveling to national gatherings of parties in other countries is another good way to establish contacts. Gradually you establish a fraternal relationship in which each side will learn from the other.

It's not merely the lectures and the resolutions

JAMES P. CANNON [1890-1974]

and the discussions; it's also the fraternity of meeting people of one's own kind—revolutionists—of different nationalities. It's a wonderful experience, a wonderful influence.

You know, the Greek Olympiad was not merely an athletic performance as it's portrayed today. It was a gathering of Greeks from all over the lands where the Greeks had established themselves, coming together to fraternize. I think the athletic performances were merely part of the show. The real thing was fraternization, personal contact.

El Socialista: We have had some contact with other Latin American comrades, and we want to develop the same kind of contact with the Socialist Workers Party, particularly in trying to incorporate some of the traditions of Trotskyism that are embodied in the Socialist Workers Party.

Cannon: I think that should be welcomed and facilitated in every possible way.

El Socialista: One of our difficulties is financial. We are a relatively small movement and most of our members and supporters have little money. This makes it hard to establish a professional staff.

We don't have the money to subsidize the full-time workers that we need. For example, right now we need a full-time editor for our paper, a full-time political secretary, and a fulltime organizational secretary. We can only raise enough money to have one of these on full-time.

I know that in the early years the North American movement also had hard financial problems. On the basis of your experiences with this problem, do you have any advice?

Cannon: Our experience was that we just suffered. We had to have fulltime workers but we didn't have the money, so one way or another we got a few full-time workers without the money. If you ask me how we did it, I can't tell you now. It's easier said than done.

It requires extraordinary effort and sometimes one or two of the comrades on staff have to go to work to pay for the rent and the groceries. Another time some comrade has to quit his job because a vacancy in the party has to be filled. There's no rule or law there. It's a question of will, determination, necessity, inspiration, and spirit and several other things.

El Socialista: I wish I could ask you a lot more questions. We're very curious to know about the discussions that you had with Trotsky and other leaders of the Comintern in the early days of the movement. There are a million other questions I wish I could ask you.

Cannon: Come again.

El Socialista: We intend to.

ALSO FROM PATHFINDER

Labor, Nature, and the Evolution of Humanity

The Long View of History

FREDERICK ENGELS
KARL MARX
GEORGE NOVACK
MARY-ALICE WATERS

Without understanding that social labor, transforming nature, has driven humanity's evolution for millions of years, working people are unable to see beyond the capitalist epoch of class exploitation that warps all human relations, ideas, and values. Only the revolutionary conquest of state power by the working class can open the door to a world free of capitalist exploitation, degradation of nature, subjugation of women, racism, and war. A world built on human solidarity. A socialist world. $12. Also in Spanish and French.

The Clintons' Anti-Working-Class Record

Why Washington Fears Working People

JACK BARNES

What working people need to know about the profit-driven course of Democrats and Republicans alike over the last three decades. And the political awakening of workers seeking to understand and resist the capitalist rulers' assaults. $10. Also in Spanish, French, Farsi, Greek.

Is Socialist Revolution in the US Possible?

A Necessary Debate Among Working People

MARY-ALICE WATERS

An unhesitating "Yes"—that's the answer given here. Possible—but not inevitable. That depends on what working people *do*. $7. Also in Spanish, French, Farsi.

The Teamster Series

FARRELL DOBBS

Four books on the strikes, organizing drives, and political campaigns that transformed the Teamsters across the Midwest in the 1930s into a militant industrial union movement. Written by Farrell Dobbs, the general organizer of these Teamster battles and leader of the Socialist Workers Party.

A tool for workers seeking to use union power in every workplace and advance the fight for an independent labor party. $16 each, series $50. Also in Spanish. *Teamster Rebellion* is also available in French, Farsi, Greek.

The Struggle for a Proletarian Party

JAMES P. CANNON

"The workers of America have power enough to topple the structure of capitalism at home and to lift the whole world with them when they rise," Cannon asserts. On the eve of World War II, a founder of the communist movement in the US and leader of the Communist International in Lenin's time defends the program and party-building norms of Bolshevism. $20. Also in Spanish and Farsi.

The Communist Manifesto

KARL MARX AND FREDERICK ENGELS

Communism, say the founding leaders of the revolutionary workers movement, is not a set of ideas or preconceived "principles" but workers' line of march to power. It springs from a "movement going on under our very eyes." $5. Also in Spanish, French, Farsi, Arabic.

EXPAND YOUR REVOLUTIONARY LIBRARY

New Edition!

Che Guevara on Economics and Politics in the Transition to Socialism

CARLOS TABLADA

It's essential for working people to win state power, said Ernesto Che Guevara. "Then there's the second stage, maybe more difficult than the first"—the transition from dog-eat-dog capitalism to socialism. That includes moving from work as a condition for survival, to voluntary social labor through which we express our common humanity. Includes Fidel Castro's 1987 speech "Che's Ideas Are Absolutely Relevant Today." New edition with substantially expanded selections from Guevara's writings. $17. Also in Spanish.

Thomas Sankara Speaks

The Burkina Faso Revolution, 1983–87

Under Sankara's guidance, Burkina Faso's revolutionary government led peasants, workers, women, and youth to expand literacy; to sink wells, plant trees, erect housing; to combat women's oppression; to carry out land reform; to join others worldwide to free themselves from the imperialist yoke. $20. Also in French.

Cuba and the Coming American Revolution

JACK BARNES

This is a book about the example set by the Cuban people that socialist revolution is not only necessary—it can be made. A book about the struggles of workers and other exploited producers in the imperialist heartland, and the youth attracted to them. About the class struggle in the US, where the revolutionary capacities of working people are as utterly discounted by the ruling powers as were those of the Cuban toilers. And just as wrongly. $10. Also in Spanish, French, Farsi.

By Any Means Necessary

MALCOLM X

"The imperialists know the only way you will voluntarily turn to the fox is to show you a wolf." In eleven speeches and interviews, Malcolm X presents a revolutionary alternative to this reformist trap, taking up political alliances, women's rights, US intervention in the Congo and Vietnam, capitalism and socialism, and more. $15

Women in Cuba: The Making of a Revolution Within the Revolution

VILMA ESPÍN
ASELA DE LOS SANTOS
YOLANDA FERRER

The integration of women in the ranks and leadership of the Cuban Revolution was intertwined with the proletarian course led by Fidel Castro from the start. This is the story of that revolution and how it transformed the women and men who made it. $17. Also in Spanish, Farsi, Greek.

New Expanded Edition!

Cosmetics, Fashion, and the Exploitation of Women

MARY-ALICE WATERS
JOSEPH HANSEN, EVELYN REED

"Norms of beauty and fashion are inseparable from the class struggle" is the new opening chapter of this timely expanded edition of a lively 1950s debate in the *Militant*, a socialist newsweekly. How cosmetics and fashion monopolies rake in profits from social insecurities of women and adolescents. Why women's integration in the workforce and unions marks a major advance in the fight for their emancipation. A Marxist classic on the origins of women's oppression and the working-class road forward. $15. Also in Spanish, French, Farsi, Greek.